God Is Looking for a Mature Man:
Where Are You, Man?

Dr. John W. Hatcher III

ISBN 978-1-63525-078-7 (Paperback)
ISBN 978-1-63525-079-4 (Digital)

Christian Faith Publishing, Inc.
296 Chestnut Street
Meadville, PA 16335
www.christianfaithpublishing.com

Printed in the United States of America

CONTENTS

Then the Lord God called to the man and said
unto him, "Where are you, Man?"

—*Genesis 3:9*

Dr. John W. Hatcher III

DEDICATION

To God be the glory! To God be all the glory! There have been times in my life when I have felt totally inadequate and unworthy, including times while writing this book, but to God be the glory! There are times when I feel like a complete failure as a man, but to God be the glory! There are times when I feel like my marriage is in trouble and my children are out of order, but to God be the glory! There are times when I feel afraid and confused, but to God be the glory! There are times when I am guilty, ashamed, and embarrassed, but to God be the glory! There are times when I have started something and didn't know how to finish it, but to God be the glory! There are times when I have asked, "How in the world did I get here?" but to God be the glory! There have been times when I have wondered why I am writing this book, but to God be all the glory! My life is not my own. I give my all to you. To you, Lord Jesus, be all the glory, all the honor, and all the praise for all the things you have done and continue to do.

I further dedicate this book to every man who desires to be in a right relationship with God. Every man who aspires to walk in his God-ordained identity and to fulfill his divine purpose. This book is dedicated to every man who endeavors to live a balanced and holy life while working for, warring for, and worshiping within his family and community.

Finally, to my son, John Wills Hatcher IV, my future sons-in-love, and all my Sons of Promise, may you come to know who you are in Jesus Christ, walk wholly in your life's purpose, and be the mature man that you are destined to be.

ACKNOWLEDGEMENTS

I am grateful to my Heavenly Father for loving me completely and unconditionally, to my biological father John Wills Hatcher Jr., my grandfathers (John Wills Hatcher Sr. and Curtis Crum Sr.) for all the love, protection, encouragement, and support you all gave me as I developed through my early years. I further acknowledge the other men who have helped to father me toward maturity as a man:

The Men That Fathered Me!

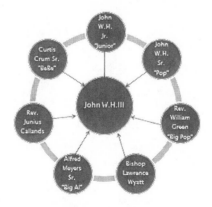

My spiritual father (Rev. Junius Callands), my father-in-love (Rev. William Green), my pastor (Bishop Lawrence Wyatt), and my Italian father (Alfred Meyers Sr.)! These men have poured into my life in a variety of ways and have helped to shape who I am today. I love, appreciate, and honor you all!

Finally, to my friend and brother Mark Swift, thank you for your encouragement during this process.

BOOK REVIEW

Dr. John Hatcher's book, *God is Looking for a Mature Man: Where are you, man?* is both timely and timeless. The book is timely because we are in the midst of a crisis in America centered on male identity. As Dr. Hatcher makes clear, we need more men to embrace their calling as fathers, mentors, brothers, and friends. The book emphasizes what it truly means to be a man, using Holy Scripture as the guidepost for his expanded definition. Dr. Hatcher challenges every male reader to take on the mantle of manhood and fulfill God's call in our lives--to be men of significance, men whose core values are grounded in God's Word. The book is timeless because it offers insights that not only provide us with insight and advice that is immediately applicable, but it also offers help and thoughts that will touch lives far into the future. Men: Buy this book. Live this book.

Dr. Carlos Campo
President, Ashland University

At a time wherein there is a deficit of full male presence in homes and millions are flowing through the penal system each year, there is a clarion call. Dr. John Hatcher is a voice from the trenches with a sound word that jolts the young man's consciousness and stimulates the older man's apathetic engagement. God is calling through the pages of this book for the desperate healing that particularly godly men can bring. Let the army of God-fearing men rise up!

Dr. Antipas L. Harris, Associate Professor at Regent University
President of GIELD, Inc.

Has there ever been a time in the history of mankind that biblical manhood has been more needed? Has there ever been a time when the loss biblical fatherhood has been more obvious? Indeed, the land is devastated due to the lack of mature men willing to teach and disciple their families, impact their communities, and lift up their local churches!

My friend, John Hatcher, nails it. Pulling no punches, John weaves a bible-base tapestry of love and purpose, hard work and joy, and Spirit-filled family discipleship as it relates to manhood and fatherhood. And right on time too!

John, out of his own experience as a husband and father, and with Scripture as his rule and guide, lays out critical principles that if studied and adhered to, will bring many men into maturity and subsequently bless their families for generations.

I'm honored to endorse this book, and more honored to call John my friend. Read it!

Bishop Carlton C. McLeod
Senior Pastor, Calvary Revival Church Chesapeake

In a society that is continually spiraling into chaos and immorality, it is clear that we are lacking strong male leaders in our homes. This book does a great job of not only asking the question "Where are the men? but goes on to systematically teach what manhood is as God designed it to be. I am more than confident that this book will help anyone seeking to learn what biblical manhood is and how we, as men, should go about our lives in a manner pleasing to God.

Don Carey III, Professional Football Player
National Football League – Detroit Lions

A Message from the Author

The purpose of this book is to provide a Godly picture of what it means to be a mature man of God in Christ Jesus. It provides a biblical basis for understanding manhood. It is intended to edify the body of Christ and to help repair the breach between *God's* best for man and the current state of man in modern society. All errors are mine; please forgive me. I have intentionally used plain language, tables, relevant images, and practical assignments to engage you, the reader, in this timely message to man. I hope that I have communicated this message with the *love* of God, the *truth* of Jesus Christ, and with the integrity of the Holy Spirit. My prayer is that this message is received in the spirit in which it has been communicated. I challenge you to examine yourself with regard to the questions related to your spiritual identity and your divine purpose, as well as the roles and responsibilities you have as a man of God. Please understand, that although it may only take a few hours, days, weeks, or months to finish reading this book, it will take a lifetime to live it out. May the love, grace, and peace of God guide your heart and mind as you engage the content of this book. All profits from the sell of this book will go toward the mission of the Sons of Promise and Daughters of Destiny Mentorship Program.

INTRODUCTION

My personal journey into maturity:

I was born in Elizabeth, New Jersey, during the fall of 1971. I am the youngest of seven children and the second born son to John Jr. and Loretta Hatcher. My parents named me John Wills Hatcher III, after my father and grandfather. I have wondered from time to time why my older brother didn't receive the name that was given to me since he was and is the firstborn son. The only conclusion that I have reached is that, who I am[1] was predetermined by God from the foundation of the world.

As a young child, I had several challenges to contend with that I believe God used to help shape who I am today. I was diagnosed with asthma prior to age two. As a toddler, I was hospitalized after a severe asthma attack. Thankfully, it was the last time I had such an extreme occasion. Another challenge I had early on was my bowed legs. You may recall the metal braces worn by the young actor in the movie *Forest Gump*. Well, between ages two and four, I had to wear similar metal braces in order to help straighten my legs. As a child, my family lived in the second court of the Migliore Manor (10E), which was a public housing project located in an area of the city called the Port. I recall, at some point, all seven of us children and my parents living in a large four-bedroom apartment. My father was a disabled veteran and my mother worked part-time at a child-care facility. Our family qualified for and received public assistance (food

---

[1]   Jeremiah 1:5

stamps); which back then you had to take the oversized monopoly-like money to the cashier.

Neither my father nor my mother completed high school; however, they fervently stressed the importance of each of their children graduating high school. Based on their own experience at the time, their goal for us was simply to graduate with a high school diploma. The expectation of continuing education and aspiring to higher education I would establish within the next generation of my family. I recall my mother taking us to church most Sundays and my father preparing our Sunday dinner. I was still very young when my two oldest sisters moved to the Bronx, New York, where my maternal grandmother and family lived. I don't recall the details of the incident that led to the move; however, I do remember my oldest sister being taken to the hospital after ingesting bleach. Our family eventually moved to Plainfield, New Jersey, where I grew up and completed my early education. I recall being in school and getting slightly above average grades. I remember being encouraged by signs in school that read, "It is cool to be smart!" and "Readers are leaders!" I looked forward to playing football and baseball in the local Pop Warner football and Little League baseball organizations respectively. I was coached and praised for my talent and efforts. However, I recall most of my encouragement coming from both parents being on the sidelines at my sporting events. When I scored my first touchdown, my team said I carried three or four guys into the end zone. I remember seeing my father out of the corner of my eye and hearing him yelling, "That is my boy!" My loving and supportive mother would most often attend parent-teacher conferences. My parents' presence was sometimes missed; however, due to our family not always having a personal vehicle for transportation. I was truly blessed to have had parents who made every attempt to provide me with such support.

My father, on occasion, would have us sit down and watch TV shows such as *The Ten Commandments* and *Roots*. These things may seem insignificant; however, they had an impact on me as a child because they provided a balance of spiritual and cultural heritage. Spiritual and cultural heritage are two pillars necessary in the training and development of every child regardless of race or socioeconomic status. Our neighborhood was somewhat quiet, and that was partly due to the graveyard across the street. I remember one of our neighbors, who worked in the cafeteria of a school, regularly bringing leftover sandwiches home and giving them to our family. My brother and I would cut grass, rake leaves, shovel snow, and make runs to the store or bakery for our neighbors. I would say that we looked out for our neighbors and our neighbors looked out for us. Along with the other young guys in our neighborhood, my brother and I would put together a football team, and we would go to the local parks to challenge other neighborhoods. Life in this respect was good.

However, like many families, not only those in poverty, everything in our family did not line up with the *Cosby Show*. I clearly recall my father being a heavy alcohol drinker to the extent that he would have been considered a functioning alcoholic. One night after driving the family home from a visit to Elizabeth, New Jersey, my father walked in the house and went up the stairs to go to bed. As he reached the top of the stairs, he lost his balance and fell backward without sobering arms or presence of mind to brace his fall. That night he severely burned his face and arms as he slid down the carpet-covered stairs. I wasn't sure if my father was going to live or die that night, but thankfully, he came through. That incident has been seared in my memory. Maybe it is a reminder of the fact that part of my early family life had some very dark secrets that would make me cringe if they were spoken of. The scars my father suffered eventually healed with no evidence of that horrible night. However, there is a scar that remains with me from the lesson of sobriety I learned from my father that night.

I was fifteen years old when I first accepted Jesus Christ into my life. I attended the City of Refuge Church in Newark, New Jersey, where the pastor was Rev. Junius Callands. I met April for the first time when I was seventeen years old at a church camp, which I didn't realize until after we had been married for about two years. After graduating high school, my father and I spent the next two months talking about the issues of life. At the end of those two months, I left for navy boot camp. Before I left, I told my father that I was going to make him proud of me and his response was, "Boy, I am already proud of you." Three weeks later, I received a letter from my father reiterating his love for me and his pride in the young man I had become. By week four of boot camp, my father had a heart attack in his sleep and died. I am eternally grateful that I was able to spend those final months with my father talking about issues related to life.

It wasn't until I was stationed overseas in Italy that I became a reader. Until that time, I could read, but I did not take pleasure in reading. At some point, I had convinced myself that I didn't like reading. After being stationed thousands of miles from home, I had this urge to understand more about African American history. I started reading books written by people of color, such as Booker T. Washington, W.E.B. Du Bois, Marcus Garvey, Alice Walker, Malcolm X, and Mahatma Gandhi. I would read books on the history of slavery in the United States. Looking back, I realized that I was becoming more and more angry about the mistreatment of those of African descent as well as the disparities between the African American communities and the broader society. I began reading the Koran and studying about Islam as a way to reject the religion offered by the dominant culture. I continued to read history books and other documents that communicated how to methodically break male slaves as if they were horses while raping and instilling fear into the hearts of female slaves and their children. After about a year of reading materials that helped to educate me about my African American heritage, the Lord spoke to me and told me not to read another book until I had completely read through the Holy Bible. By this time, I was reading anywhere from one to three hours daily. As I engaged the scriptures I would get tired and sleepy until I started to draw connections with the people and stories. The struggles of the Israelites I would relate to the plight of African Americans in the United States. In my mind, I drew connections between characters, such as Moses and Martin Luther King Jr. I remember being excited about the journey of discovery that I was on. By the time I had completely read through the Bible, I felt a change in my outlook on life. I was not as angry and I felt like I had found some sense of who I was and where I belonged.

The Eagle Story

April and I were married four months after I left active duty, and we began growing our family. Shortly after our first anniversary, we had our firstborn (Janae), and within four years, we had our three oldest daughters (to include Janine and Janette). By our seventh anniversary, we had all five of our children (adding John IV and Jasmine).

I was the first member of my immediate family to attend college, and I began to do so while in the US Navy. I had completed my first associate degree by the time I was discharged from active duty and I used my GI bill to complete my bachelor of arts degree in health and physical education with my teaching certification. I began my career in education as a substitute teacher by day and a substitute custodian in the evenings. In 1998, after being honorably discharged from the US Navy I began teaching full-time. I taught for a few years before I completed my master of arts degree in education administration and supervision in December 2001. After ten years of working in the classroom, I became a public school administrator; which is what I currently do. I realized that my passion to teach was still greater than my knowledge and skills to engage the teaching and learning process. I needed to fly higher, and I needed to go deeper.

In January of 2004, I was participating in a worship service at our local church when I heard the spirit of God speak to my heart and say, "Fly, eagle, fly…you shall mount up with wings like eagles… Fly, eagle, fly!" These words were repeated a number of times. That night, I told my wife what I heard the Spirit of God say to me. I must interject the fact that at this point in my life, I had been collecting eagle symbols for about five years, so in my mind, there was no doubt that this message was for me. In May of 2004, my family and I went to visit some friends in Pennsylvania from New Jersey. We stayed for the weekend and had a nice time. As we prepared to leave early Sunday afternoon, we went down to the nearby lake and stood around talking for a little while. While we were engaged in our conversation, I noticed a bird flying across the lake, and I remember saying to myself, "That is an eagle." As the bird flew closer and closer, I gave it more and

21

more attention. It got just about in front of where we were and I said, "That is a falcon," and it suddenly swooped down to get a fish. As it swooped down, it turned its tail toward us and I could see clearly that it was an eagle. Once again, the words from that previous message came back to me, "Fly, eagle, fly...you shall mount up with wings like eagles...Fly, eagle, fly!" I reminded my wife of the words that were spoken to me by the Spirit of God back in January of that year. Now my wife and I had been planning to go to Hawaii for our tenth wedding anniversary in August 2004. This would be the honeymoon that we didn't have the opportunity to take initially due to financial constraints. Our children were still very young, and we were blessed to save enough to take each of them along with us. As we arrived in

Hawaii and settled in our resort, we decided to take a ride in order to schedule a luau. As we were riding along the highway of the Big Island, there were these black lava rocks with messages written on them with white mineral rocks from the ocean. I noticed one of the messages read, "Fly, eagles, fly," and I got really excited while driving. My wife did not see the message, so I looked around for landmarks and decided to take a picture on the way back. We stopped and took the picture after scheduling the luau, and it was clear to us that the Lord was telling us that it was time for us to spread our wings. By October

2004 we had our home on the market, and by December 2004, our home was sold and we had a contract on our new home in Virginia. We moved to Virginia in August 2005, and by February 2006, I was enrolled in the doctoral program for Educational Leadership at Regent University. I completed my doctorate in December 2011.

During the early part of my life, I never thought of becoming a doctor of any sort. Ironically enough, the night I completed my final defense for my doctorate, my family and I celebrated. We were around the table and my children were discussing what type of doctor they were going to become. This took me back to my parents who wanted more for my siblings and me than what they themselves had attained. I have completed my twenty-second year working in public education in June 2015, and by God's grace, I am currently in my twenty-second year of a God-centered marriage with my beautiful and forgiving wife, April. Who by the way, would probably modify the title of this book to read, "God Is Looking for a Mature Man—and so Is My Wife!" I have had the opportunity to teach at the university level, and I look forward to starting a private Christian boarding school for at-risk males. In my personal and professional life, I have experienced many challenges and failures, as well as victories and triumphs.[2] I have discovered that in this maturation process, experiencing trials

---

[2]   James 1:4

and tests are inevitable, yet I also understand that I am more than a conqueror through Christ. I understand the common meaning of the word *maturity* is the following:

> **ma·tur·i·ty**[3] (mə-tyoor'ĭ-tē, -toor'-, -choor'-)
> *n. pl.* **ma·tur·i·ties** is:
> **1. a.** The state or quality of being fully grown or developed.

The revelation that I now have and the definition I am using for this context is that *maturity* is the *result of drawing closer to God; it is when one's spiritual identity and life purpose come into alignment with the call of God on one's life.* As men, we need to experience maturity in every aspect of our lives. I can see the evidence of maturity manifesting itself in my life and at the same time I see areas where continued growth and development are still needed. I am communicating this message with the desire to truly be an example of a mature man in Christ. At age forty-four, I am beyond the fullness of physical maturity and I need to focus on things such as eating healthy and overcoming the challenge of maintaining my ideal weight. Mentally, I have acquired a terminal degree in the area of my calling, yet I must continue to strive to allow the Word of Christ[4] to richly abide in my heart and mind…and live it! Socially, I have reached a milestone of twenty-two years of marriage, and again, my wife would agree that sometimes she is looking for a mature husband. All five of my children are honor students, and we are bringing them up in the fear and admonition of the Lord, yet I still make mistakes as I resolve who I am as a father. I have received a state certification in conflict resolution, but I still fail at times to express my feelings in the most effective and loving way. I have worked since I was twelve years old, I am a tithe payer, I am a cheerful giver, and I have been debt free; however, I have accumulated some ill-advised debts and although I

---

[3]   http://www.yourdictionary.com/maturityes
[4]   Colossians 3:16

am an ordained minister of the gospel of Jesus Christ, I still sin and fall short of God's best for my life.

This information is being shared with you the reader to expose where I am. As the author of this book, I am sharing with you some insights into my life story, my journey in this maturation process, and yes, my shortcomings. I made the decision to share a part of my personal story not for you to know me and certainly not for you to judge where I am but to release you to examine yourself. I encourage you in the name of Jesus Christ to assess your own life and consider the questions that are presented in the body of this text. God said to Job, "Brace yourself like a man; because I have some questions for you, and you must answer them."[5] Let us come out of hiding, brothers, and step out into the glory of the Lord and walk the path He has ordered for each of our lives. In Jesus's name I pray. Amen!

---

[5]   Job 38:3

CHAPTER 1

Where Are You, Man?

Then the LORD *God called to Adam and said to him,*
"Where are you?"[6]

"Where are you, man?" This question is asked in the context of today's society as many men find themselves struggling to adequately address the various roles and responsibilities given to their charge by our creator God. The instructions for how to live were given to man in the beginning of time and established from the foundation of the world. In order for a man to accurately and truthfully respond to this question, he must first understand the intent of the question. God is asking man this question now, as He did with Adam, not

---

because He doesn't know the answer to the question.[7] Our creator God is omniscient or omniscience, meaning He is all-knowing.[8] God is posing this question to every man in order to challenge us to reflect on where we are in our relationship with Him, as well as the identity and purpose that He has called us to. The answer to this question is not a matter of location, as in your current living address or your GPS coordinates; neither is it referring to your socioeconomic status or any position or title you may hold. However, the question is intended to challenge every man to examine his personal relationship with our Heavenly Father and the call of God on his life. Within the body of this text, you (the reader) are presented with this question and others in order for you to ponder where you are in your walk with God.[9] You can assess where you are in the maturation process, which involves the discovery of your spiritual identity, as well as the fulfillment of your life's purpose. It also requires you to meditate on this question with regard to living a well-balanced and holy lifestyle. Where are you in regard to the fulfillment of your duties and responsibilities as a man? This question is the central theme that runs throughout the pages of this book. So, let us go back to the beginning as we begin to peel back the layers of life and living discussed in the context of this question posed to man.

Created in Love

Love is God and God is love; *it is the source of all that exists.*[10] In the beginning, God created the heavens and the earth as a habitat for His masterpiece to dwell. The first five and one-half days were all strategic in that God's design was to create a setting for His grand plan for man to unfold. Man was created out of the abundance of God's love. God worked, planned, and prepared the world for man to live in His good pleasure. After preparing the heavens and the earth, the Lord God created man in His image and in His likeness.

---

7 1 Cor. 11:28: "Let a man examine himself…"
8 1 John 3:20c: "So to be omniscient means that God is all knowing."
9 Job 38:3: "Brace yourself like a man…I have some questions for you."
10 1 John 4:8

Then God said, "Let us make man in our image, after our likeness. And let them have dominion over the fish of the sea and over the birds of the heavens and over the livestock and over all the earth and over every creeping thing that creeps on the earth. So God created man in his own image, in the image of God he created him; male and female he created them."[11]

When a man and woman are intimate and they come together in love, they can potentially create a new life as the triune Godhead did in the beginning. One of the first things that a father will do when his child is born is to examine the child looking for a resemblance of the child to himself. He is looking for those features that represent the love and life connections between himself and his child. We were created in the unconditional love of God and with an established covenant and connection to our Heavenly Father. A covenant is the most intimate relationship type and is established by a spoken vow. As a husband and wife make a vow and unite in the creation of a new life (divine order), so too the Godhead took counsel in the spirit realm to create man. A husband and wife become one in love; as a result, the woman and the seed become one, and the result is the covenant family unit. The covenant family unit is emblematic of the Holy Trinity, which is made up of God the Father, God the Son in the person of Jesus the Christ, and God the Holy Spirit.

After creating Adam in His image, God placed His masterpiece "man" in the context of the garden that He prepared and provided in order to sustain man's life and fellowship with Himself. He gave Adam specific instructions to tend to the garden, which speaks to the responsibilities of man in his home. God charges every man to attend to the affairs of his household by planting and watering his seeds, growing the flowers and trees while also pruning and weeding the garden of his home. These expectations are expressed through

---

[11]   Genesis 1:26 and 27

love by the man who nurtures his family and maintains godly order in his home and garden.

> *And the* LORD *God took the man, and put him into the garden of Eden to dress it and to keep it. And the* LORD *God commanded the man, "You are free to eat from any tree in the garden; [17] but you must not eat from the tree of the knowledge of good and evil, for when you eat from it you will certainly die."*[12]

These commands were given to help man remain in a safe place with Father God and to help Adam avoid being separated from Him as a result of his failure to heed the commandment. God's intention was for man to represent Him in the earth and to rule over it as He ruled the heavens.

> *And God blessed them. And God said to them, "Be fruitful and multiply and fill the earth and subdue it, and have dominion over the fish of the sea and over the birds of the heavens and over every living thing that moves on the earth."*[13]

God so loved man that he ordained him with glory and honor and placed him in charge of His creation. God created man with a will, which means man, unlike any other creation has a choice. The scripture states,

> *What is man that you are mindful of them, human beings that you care for them, You made them a little lower than the angels; you crowned them with glory and honor. You made them rulers over the works of your hands; you put everything under their feet.*[14]

---

[12]   Genesis 2:15–17
[13]   Genesis:28
[14]   Psalms 8:4–6

God's love for man is perfected toward us, and His desire is that we would walk wholly in the identity and purpose that He uploaded in each of us from the foundation of the world.

Fall to Fear

Adam and Eve were in the garden when the serpent enticed the woman to eat from the tree of the knowledge of good and evil, and Eve in turn shared the fruit with her husband. As a result, their eyes were opened, and man was able to see his nakedness, and he was consumed with fear. Adam and Eve covered themselves because of the shame and guilt they were experiencing as a result of Adam's failure to obey the instructions given to him by God.

Shame is the *dishonor, disgrace, and embarrassment that a person might feel when their sin or wrong doing comes to light.* I have been there a few times before. Shame can be extremely damaging because it is usually accompanied by doubt. Doubt causes one to question what they believe, who they are, and where they are. We know that the scriptures say that without faith it is impossible to please God.[15] I perceive that many men struggle in their relationship with God because they have not been able to overcome the shame and doubt of their past. One of the church mothers in my home church in New Jersey came up with a formula that she would often share about spiritual nourishment. She would say, "Feed your faith, and starve your doubt!"

Guilt is the *feeling a person might experience when they are at fault; it is blame assigned to one who has engaged in a wrongful act; a feeling one receives when he fails to meet the established expectations; and it is a negative response to a developmental crisis.* Adam was guilty of not following the specific instructions that God had given him concerning the tree in the middle of the garden. Not only was Adam at fault, but he did not want to take responsibility for his wrongful act. This may sound familiar to some of us. Guilt is a self-judging

---

[15]   Hebrew 11:6

feeling that opens the door to a destructive type of fear; which will cause one to lose sight and separate from grace, mercy, and love.

Fear is *a spirit that is contrary to love.* Like darkness is to light, fear can (if allowed to) cause someone to hide from the true light of love. Although Adam was created in the image of God, his sons were created in his image because Adam separated himself from God and, in doing so, created a counterculture rooted in fear. Therefore, all the decedents of Adam have been introduced to fear through his sin of disobedience. The scripture says, "We were born into sin and shaped in iniquity."[16]

Adam opened the door to *sin*, which is being defined as "any action that is contrary to God's instructions, commandments, and ordinances." Adam heard the voice of the Lord calling in the garden, and he hid himself out of fear, "Where are you?"[17] questioned the Lord. Adam was afraid because of his sin of disobedience against God the Father. So, not only was he experiencing shame and guilt, but now he was afraid and separated himself from a loving God; which opened the door to sickness and death. Adam responded to God's call by saying,

> *"I heard you in the garden, and I was afraid because I was naked; so I hid." And He (God) said, "Who told you that you were naked? Have you eaten from the tree that I commanded you not to eat from?" The man (Adam) said, "The woman you put here with me—she gave me some fruit from the tree, and I ate it."*[18]

Adam was afraid as he engaged this dialogue with the Lord and began to charge God for his own disobedience. Adam failed to take responsibility for his actions again in his next breath and thrusts the blame on Eve. Now, I am not sure how long after the first seven days that this occurrence took place; however, I do know that

---

[16]   Psalms 51:5
[17]   Genesis 3:9
[18]   Genesis 3:10–12

particular day was a terrible day for man. The day Adam disobeyed the Lord's instruction set a precedent for things to come. That one act of disobedience by Adam led to the fall of mankind and opened the door to sin, fear, shame, guilt, and ultimately death. All of which are contrary to what God originally intended for man. *Death*, in this context, simply means "the separation of man from a loving creator God and His divine order," which is the first death.

The Consequence

As a result of man's disobedience, the serpent, Eve, and Adam all received a disposition from God:

- The serpent was cursed above all livestock and was sentenced to crawl on its belly and eat dust all the days of its life. The Lord put hostility between the serpent and the woman, as well as, her offspring (*this point is crucial in chapter 3 when we discuss hedges of love, protection, encouragement, and support*).[19] The head of the serpent will be struck by the heel of the woman.
- The woman was sentenced to endure severe pain during her pregnancy and the delivery of her children. In addition, her desire would be toward her husband and he would rule over her.
- The ground was cursed because of Adam, and from that moment, he was sentenced to work a contaminated ground. Man was punished to toil all the days of his life as he ate of the earth and worked by the sweat of his brow; he would do so until he returned to the ground from which he came.

I can imagine that during that time, all the oceans were crystal clear, the air and atmosphere were pure and most suitable for breathing, and man was truly in his prime. The things initiated

---

[19]   Genesis 3:15

by Adam's sin are manifested in the world today and the decline of man and his habitat are evident. All across the world, oceans and waterways are polluted, the air that many of us breathe daily does almost as much harm as it does good (in some places), and very few people are living out their allotted 120 years. Illnesses began to manifest themselves as mankind and his habitation started to decline. The genetically modified organisms (GMOs) in many food products are causing an increase in diseases, such as, irritable bowel syndrome, cancer, asthma, and more. These negative effects are the consequences of man's original sin.

> *But sin, seizing the opportunity afforded by the commandment, produced in me every kind of coveting. For apart from the law, sin was dead. Once I was alive apart from the law; but when the commandment came, sin sprang to life and I died.* [20]

It was previously mentioned that sin is any action that is contrary to God's instructions for man and also that it caused man to be afraid and separate himself from God. God loves man and desires to be in fellowship with him. This is why God asked Adam where he was after he had eaten the forbidden fruit. I believe God wanted to restore Adam immediately; however, Adam went and hid himself. I don't see where Adam repented for his disobedience, so God issued a consequence and He still gave man a way out through His mercy, grace, love, and ultimately His son Jesus Christ.

> *The first man Adam became a living being"; the last Adam became a life-giving spirit. But it is not the spiritual that is first but the natural, and then the spiritual. The first man was from the earth, a man of dust; the second man is from heaven. As was the man of dust, so also are those who are of the dust, and as is the man of heaven, so also are those who are of heaven. Just*

---

[20]   Roman 7:8 and 9

as we have bourne the image of the man of dust, we shall
also bear the image of the man of heaven.[21]

The Current State of Man

Just as everyone dies because we all belong to Adam,
everyone who belongs to Christ will be given new life.[22]

Every thought we entertain, every word we speak, every decision
we make, every action we take, every belief we have in this life is
either rooted in *love* or it is rooted in *fear*. Many of us were taught
that the opposite of *love* is hate. I am suggesting to you that the
opposite of love is not hate but fear and that hate is only a by-product
of fear. We also need to distinguish between the fear of God that is
based in love and comes with a sense of reverence and awe; which
happens to be a form of worship. This was the original form of fear
that God intended for man to have. The fear that came out of Adam's
sin is a perverted fear. The latter form is a fear that came as a result
of sin and disobedience; it also gave way to all types of illnesses and
even death. This type of fear is produced from the sinful nature and
it is contrary to love. It has caused many of us to separate ourselves
from God as Adam did when he hid himself in the garden. In my
experience, some of the major fears that men struggle with today are
the following:

1. The fear of not being loved
2. The fear of being rejected or hurt; and
3. The fear of failure

What all this means is that we choose to lay a foundation for our
lives and set the course for our destiny rooted in either love or fear.
However, many men today have chosen (whether we will admit it

---

21 1 Cor. 15:45–49
22 1 Cor. 15:22

or not) to once again hide from love. We must choose to repent and return to our first love and reestablish the relationship that our creator God intended for us from the foundation of this world. The following scriptures and table are used here in support of this very critical point:

1 John 4:8 – *He that loves not does not know God for God is love.*

1 John 4:18 – *There is no fear in love; but perfect love casts out fear: because fear has torment. He that fears is not made perfect in love.*

2 Timothy 1:7 – *For God hath not given us the spirit of fear; but of power, and of love, and of a sound mind.*

The Foundation of *Love*	The Foundation of *Fear*
Intimacy with God	Separation from God
Sonship	Sinner
Spiritual Identity (Jer. 1:5)	Identity Crisis (James 1:8)
Fulfillment of Purpose (Matthew 28:19 and 20)	Misguided/Unrealized Potential (Hosea 4:6)
Wholeness (John 5:14)	Brokenness (Isaiah 65:14)
Balanced Living (3 John:2)	Chaotic Lifestyle (1 John 4:18)
Needs met/Crises Resolved (Philippians 4:19)	Deficits and Deficiencies (Daniel 5:27)
Truth (John 8:32)	Lies (Proverbs 19:9)
Worker, Warrior, and Worshiper (John 4:24)	Dormant, Defeated, and Despair (Psalms 37:8)

John Eldredge (2009) made the following statement concerning the condition of man in modern society:

> What we have now is a world of uninitiated men. Partial men. Boys, mostly, walking around in men's bodies, with men's jobs and families, finances, and

responsibilities. The passing on of masculinity was never completed, if it was begun at all. The boy was never taken through the process of masculine initiation. That is why most of us are Unfinished Men. And therefore unable to truly live as men in whatever life throws at us. And unable to pass on to our sons and daughters what they need to become whole and holy men and women themselves.[23]

I believe this statement is extremely powerful and extremely accurate in its depiction of where many men are in our private and sometimes even our public lives. Eldredge's (2009) statement provides us insight as to why many people in our society have unmet needs and are struggling in many ways. The various social ills that exist in our lives, homes, and communities are the result of "partial" or "unfinished" men. Problems such as the following:

- A culture of disrespect
- Abortion rates
- Abuse (all types—mental, emotional, physical, sexual)
- Anxiety
- Broken families
- Divorce rates
- Dropout rates
- Emotional disorders
- Fatherlessness
- Gang activity
- Gender identity crisis
- Identity development crisis
- Illegal drug use and abuse
- Incarceration rates
- Life expectancy rates
- Low academic achievement rates

---

[23]   John Eldredge (2009) *Fathered by God: Learning What Your Dad Could Never Teach You.*

- Low self-esteem
- Mental illness
- Murder rates
- Physical ailments
- Poverty rates
- Sexually transmitted infections
- Single-parent homes
- Spiritual identity crisis
- Suicide rates
- Teen pregnancy rates
- The rate of violence
- Unemployment rates
- Many more.

Many men are struggling with who they are; they are having trouble with fulfilling their responsibilities and walking in their life's purpose. I believe that many of these alarming quality of life indicators are the result of men not being in their rightful place in God, in their homes, in their families, and in their communities. The maturity of men (*or the lack thereof*) is an urgent matter in today's society and it needs to be addressed. In other words, I believe that this quandary is the root cause of many of the ills that are prevalent in today's society. Our society is in decline as a result of men who have failed to live up to their duties, their responsibilities, and fulfillment of the purpose for which they have been called by God. So, I submit to you that just as God is looking for a mature man, our wives are looking for mature men, our children need to be fathered by mature men, our communities need leaders who are mature men, and this world needs mature men who will rise up and name the name of Jesus Christ. Once again, I encourage you in the name of Jesus to assess your own life and consider the questions that are presented in the body of this text. God said to Job, *"Brace yourself like a man; because I have some questions for you, and you must answer them."*[24] Let us come out of hiding brothers and step out into the glory of the Lord and walk the

---

[24] Job 38:3

path the Lord has ordered for each of our lives. Second Chronicles 7:14 is helpful for man's understanding, and it states, *"If My people, who are called by my name would humble themselves and pray and seek My face and turn from their wicked ways, then I will hear from heaven and will forgive their sin and heal their land."*[25]

My brothers, do you understand covenant relationships? What are you doing in order to draw closer to God the Father? Are you seeking after God in every area of your life? Are you successful in some aspects of your life and falling short in others? Have you discovered your truest identity in Christ Jesus and the call of God on your life? Are you tired of feeling ashamed and guilty of your secret sins? Will you be made whole? What would it mean to you, your family, and your community if you were whole? I mean genuinely and completely whole in God the Father? Would it impact how you develop and maintain your body, your mind, and your relationships; how you manage your time, talents, and finances; how you engage your ministry; subdue your passions, use your gifts, and pursue your purpose in life? There are too many of us who have wasted time and energy falling short of the standards of holiness, including myself. God has a solution, and the fact that you are engaging this book right now is an indication that God is calling you out. He has a specific message to deliver to you, man! Are you willing to come out of your proverbial hiding, examine where you are, discover your God-given identity, and begin taking the necessary steps toward fulfillment of your divine purpose? Before you answer these questions, understand that this will require you to take off all the coverings—every title, all the past hurts, any hidden sins—and face all your fears while standing naked before a Holy God!

When we wake up out of our sleep there are some hygiene and grooming needs that are required in order to present the desired image. We look at ourselves in the mirror: we wash, we brush, we comb, we shave, we floss, etc. For a man to look at himself in the mirror of God's word is a very challenging task. We experience some spiritual halitosis (bad breath) through the negative words we speak, a

---

[25]   2 Chronicles 7:14

sinful body odor due to the deeds done in our bodies, and the lustful beams found in the eyes of men. It is okay because you are waking up. There is some preparing that needs to take place so that we can walk in the image, identity, and purpose that God has ordained for each of our lives. But first we must awaken to the fact that there is a need for so many godly men who are genuinely seeking holiness in Christ to reexamine the life we live. God's alarm is sounding. He is pulling back the covers, and He is demanding that we come out of our hiding place and out of the slumber of sin and mediocrity. We need to stand in the mirror of God's word and ARMOR UP!

God's grace can change your future if you allow yourself to receive it, because it is only by God's grace that I deliver this message. We have a tendency to become defensive when our loved ones, or anyone else for that matter, begin to point out our faults. Without understanding grace, we perceive that they are trying to put us down and/or we fear that they will possibly love us less. God communicates His grace toward us through His son Jesus Christ when He says, "I will remember your sins no more."[26] Any Christian believer who attempts to share the truth of God must do so with grace and in the spirit of love. In other words, they must *tell the truth in love*. It is by His grace, the love of Christ, and the leading of the Holy Spirit that I share this message with my fellow Christian brothers and sisters.

So, where are the mature men called by God for this generation?[27] Where are the men after God's own heart? Where are you, husbands, who have vowed to love your wives as Christ loves the church? Where are the fathers who will love, protect, encourage, support, train, and affirm their children? Where are the mature men who will lead their families in worship and service to the Most High God? Where are the mature men who will establish organizations that will meet the needs found within our communities? The voice of God is calling out to you now, *"Where are you, man?"* It is time to lay down the guilt, shame, and fear that has caused many of us to go into hiding. I pray in the name of Jesus the Christ that you receive this message

---

[26]   Hebrew 8:12
[27]   Genesis 3:9

in the spirit of love and with the faith imparted to you by our eternal Father. Understanding that faith is a life style and that a just man lives by faith and his faith will make him whole. Finally, Jesus gave the command to lose that man (*the mature man*) and let him go.[28] Let us go, men! Let us once again draw close to our Heavenly Father and reestablish our foundations in Love! In Jesus' name, amen!

---

[28]   John 11:44

CHAPTER 2

What Is Your Relationship with Our Creator, God?

Then God said, "Let Us make man in Our image, according to Our likeness; let them have dominion over the fish of the sea, over the birds of the air, and over the cattle, over all the earth and over every creeping thing that creeps on the earth." ^{27} *So God created man in His own image; in the image of God He created him; male and female He created them. Then God blessed them, and God said to them, "Be fruitful and multiply; fill the earth and subdue it; have dominion over the fish of the sea, over the birds of the air, and over every living thing that moves on the earth."*

The Structure and Dimensions of the Tabernacle

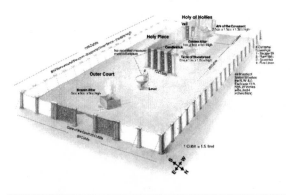

Man's relationship with God

In an attempt to illustrate where man is in his relationship with God, I am going to use the order of the tabernacle outlined in scripture[29] to describe the relationship types I propose a man can have with our creator God. God gave Moses detailed instructions on how to set up the tabernacle, which was to be a temporary dwelling place for the Shekinah Glory of God. The tent was divided into three spaces with designated articles and furniture. Each space will represent one of the relationship types to be discussed, while the fourth relationship type will represent those outside of the tabernacle. The four relationship types we will examine in this chapter that a man can have with our creator God are the unrepented sinner, the casual son, the committed son, and the covenant son. Man's position in reference to the tabernacle is an indication of what his relationship is with God the Father.

Given Adam's fall to sin, the first relationship type man has with God is positioned outside of the tabernacle. This relationship type is that of the *unrepented* sinner. The scripture found in Psalm 51:5 reads, "For I was born a sinner—yes, from the moment my mother conceived me."[30] The unrepented sinner is the only relationship type that is out of fellowship with God. Meaning, in this state man's relationship with God is nonexistent because he is out of fellowship with God, and as a result he is positioned outside of the tabernacle. He is outside of the "ark of safety." The unrepented sinner is living contrary to the will of God and either knowingly or unknowingly has not decided to turn toward God and accept Jesus Christ as his Lord and Savior.

The next three relationship types discussed in this chapter are inside the tabernacle and they represent man in fellowship with God. In these three relationship types man is considered to be inside the tabernacle and members of the body of Jesus Christ.[31] In order for

---

29   Exodus 26
30   Psalms 51:5
31   Roman 10:10, "For it is with your heart that you believe and are justified, and it is with your mouth that you profess your faith and are saved."

man to be in fellowship with God one must fulfill the scriptures found in John Chapter one verse twelve that says, "But as many as received him [Jesus], to them gave he the power to become the sons of God, even to them that believe on his name."[32] When man believes in God, receives God into his heart, and confesses that Jesus Christ is Lord of his life he enters into fellowship with God as a son. Hence, the second relationship type is that of the *casual son*, which is represented in the tabernacle by the outer court. This relationship is the result of man *hearing* the words of faith found in Romans 10:17, which states, "So faith comes from hearing, and hearing by the word of Christ."[33] A man hearing the words of Christ, repenting of his sins at the altar of God, and washing at the laver. Although man is now in fellowship with God, God's desire is always that man would draw closer to Him and not remain casual with Him.

The third relationship type is the *committed son*,[34] and it is represented in the tabernacle by the inner court also known as the holy place. The committed son has passed through the outer court and is working out his own soul salvation with fear and trembling as he moves from the outer court into the inner court.[35] The spiritual senses at work in the Holy Place are one's sense of *taste*, one's ability to *see*, and the sense of *smell*. Taste and see that the *Lord* is good; blessed is the one who takes refuge in Him. The sense of taste is at work when men eat from the bread of life and partake of the fruit of the spirit in his daily walk. The illustration of the bread and the demonstration of the fruits in a man's life are the evidence that he has tasted the bread of life from the table of shewbread. The ability to see is accomplished when one's direction in life is guided by the Holy Spirit of God and that portion of faith given to each man. The sense of sight refers to the revelation, illumination, and guidance

---

[32]   John 1:12
[33]   Romans 10:17
[34]   Psalms 34:8; Ephesians 5:2; Gal. 5:22-23; John 6:35; Psalms 119:105; Matthew 6:22; James 1:25; Psalms 141:2; Revelations 8:4
[35]   Philippians 2:12: "Therefore, my dear friends, as you have always obeyed-- not only in my presence, but now much more in my absence--continue to work out your salvation with fear and trembling.

that comes through engaging the word of God. Psalm 105:119 says, "Thy word is a lamp unto my feet and a light unto my path." Jesus Christ becomes man's guide as he continues to draw man closer to God from the light of the candlestick. The sense of smell is exercised as man offers up sincere prayers and acceptable offerings which are emblematic of one experiencing God through communion at the altar of incense (also known as the golden altar). These prayers and offerings become a sweet aroma in God's nostrils as they are lifted up toward the heavens. The committed son draws closer to God, yet there is still room for him to draw closer to our Heavenly Father.

The fourth relationship type is that of the covenant son and it is represented in the tabernacle by sanctum sanctorum or "the holy of holies." The *covenant son* has repented of his sin, matured from the outer court through the inner court, and finally he has gone beyond the veil into the most Holy place where the presence of God is. The covenant son is positioned where he can *touch* God the Father because, he worships the Lord in spirit and in truth.[36] The covenant son develops the type of relationship with God the Father that God Himself desires of all his children. God desires that all his children would draw close to Him. He desires that a mature son would touch His heart in an intimate way. In order to make the point about the importance of an intimate touch, we can use the woman who pressed through the crowd to touch the hem of Jesus's garment. There is a yearning that the covenant son has to remain close to Father God. The covenant son also understands that he is an heir and joint heir to the promises of God with our Lord Jesus Christ. The table below helps to illustrate man's relationships to God in response to the question, "Where are you, man?" as it relates to the tabernacle. It also gives an indication of the spiritual senses at work based on the

---

[36]   John 4:23–24: "But the hour cometh, and now is, when the true worshippers shall worship the Father in spirit and in truth: for the Father seeketh such to worship him. God is a Spirit: and they that worship him must worship him in spirit and in truth."

      Hebrews 12:28: "Therefore, since we are receiving a kingdom that cannot be shaken, let us be thankful, and so worship God acceptably with reverence and awe."

type of relationship, as well as, the authors estimation of the average church population.

Summary of Relationship Types

Relationship Types	In fellowship w/ God	Position to/in the Tabernacle	Spiritual Sense/s at Work	Est. % of Church
Unrepented sinner	No	Outside of the tabernacle	None	20–25*
Casual Son	Yes	Outer court	Hearing	50-55*
Committed son	Yes	Inner court	Hearing, Taste, Sight, and Smell	20-25*
Covenant son	Yes	Holy of holies	Hearing, Taste, Sight, Smell, and Touch	5–10*

*These estimates are based solely on the authors experience and are only presented as an opinion.

An explanation of the four relationship types through the order of marriage

In order to summarize the four relationship types discussed in this section, I will use the analogy of a young man seeking to espouse a young lady. Before the young man meets or is introduced to the young lady and even before he realizes his interests in her, he would be as the *unrepented* sinner not having established any relationship or connection with the young lady. Usually the young man, at this point, knows very little if anything at all about the young lady. As introductions are made and the two individuals begin to interact with each other in a very casual way, connections are made. When the young man discovers his feelings and desires toward her and she does likewise, they begin to court (the outer court) or date. As they are courting and getting to know each other they begin to draw closer and seek to take their relationship to the next level. The young man shares his desire to be committed to the young lady and he will ask for her hand in marriage. Ideally, he has discussed his intentions with the young lady's father beforehand and received his approval. When and if she accepts he should give her a ring; which is to signify that they are engaged or affianced. The ring represents their *commitment* to be married to each other (the inner court). The young man and the young woman will use this time of engagement to get to know each other in a much deeper way and hopefully through wise counsel. At some point, the wedding date is set and the two individuals make a vow to each other.[37] Once the vows are exchanged before God and a crowd of witnesses, the two enter into a *covenant* relationship with each other as husband and wife.

A covenant relationship is the most intimate type of relationship one can ever hope to experience. It is also the only relationship type where the young man is justified or has Godly permission to become one with the young lady in the most intimate way. Marriage; however, is not the only covenant relationship yet, it provides an example in the process of men drawing closer to God.[38] Relationships such as parent and child, sibling to sibling, and friend to friend are also designed to be at the covenant level of intimacy. The Bible gives the example of Jonathan and David who had a covenant relationship as friends.[39] It is extremely important for a man to understand the needs, values, and purposes of covenant relationships and to fulfill the responsibilities and trust granted to these most sacred relationships.

A dear friend, neighbor, and covenant brother of mine, Dr. Innocence Onuniwu, who in my opinion, is a great example of a mature man, shared some cultural insights from his Nigerian heritage

---

[37] Eccl. 5:5
[38] James 4:8
[39] 1 Samuel 18:3

that helped to shed light on the institution of marriage, as well as, other covenant relationships established within their communities. He explained that in the Nigerian community, marriage is held in very high regard and the divorce rate in his estimation is less than five percent. Dr. Onuniwu attributes the low divorce rate to two key variables. The two key variables that he spoke of were the children's upbringing and the societal expectations of their community.

The children's upbringing is based on respect for parents, respect for elders, and respect for authority. Children do not call their parents by their first name, and they would not look eye to eye with an adult out of respect. The man of the house is seen as the king, and his queen demonstrates respect for her husband. The man is seen as the provider, the protector, and the leader of the family. A man who is unable to provide for his family is seen as useless. The elders in the community are held in high regard, and they are seen as members of the family. A child who disrespects an elder or their parents could receive a form of corporal punishment. Children do not talk back to adults unless they are being asked a question. In addition, children are taught to respect authority, such a teachers, police officers, spiritual leaders. Disrespect at any level is unacceptable and is enforced even among young peer groups. Older siblings and cousins are also given a higher level of respect that is acknowledged by the younger siblings. The second important variable that impacts marriage is societal expectations. Meaning, because the entire family and community are invested in the marriage, the couple can bring shame upon the family and community if they were to divorces. Marriage is sacred and the family and community have a lot of influence because of their investment. These elements of the culture help to shape "who we are" Dr. Onuniwu declared as he went on to describe the process that takes place prior to the marriage ceremony (see appendix C). The process of a man and a women coming together in holy matrimony illustrates to some degree the process by which man moves through the tabernacle as he draws closer in his relationship with God. God desires for the mature man to be in covenant with Him and in the most intimate relationship as he transitions from being an unrepented sinner, to a casual son, to a committed son, and ultimately to a covenant son.

Important questions to reflect on from this chapter:

The following questions are designed to help you begin to assess where you are in your own relationship with God: Are you an un-repented sinner or are you a Son of God? If you are a Son of God, then where are you specifically in the tabernacle? Are you in the outer court, the inner court, or the Holy of Holies? Are there any spiritual senses at work in your life? What is the evidence of these senses operating in your life? What are the spiritual senses that you need to develop further in your life?

_____

_____

_____

_____

_____

_____

_____

_____

As a covenant Son of God I encourage you *man*, in the name of Jesus Christ, to rise up and assume the position established for you from the foundation of the world and began to exercise the authority given to you by our Heavenly Father.

Prayer: Father God in the name of your son Jesus Christ, I pray that you will continue to prick at the hearts of men everywhere as we draw closer to you. This is my earnest prayer in Jesus' name, Amen!

CHAPTER 3

Who Are You, Man?

Before I formed you in the womb I knew you; Before you were born I sanctified you; I ordained you a prophet to the nations."[40]

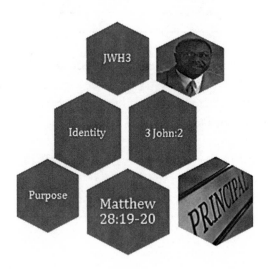

In the beginning of time, the triune Godhead took counsel in eternity to make man. God said, *"Let us make mankind in our image, in our likeness, so that they may rule over the fish in the sea and the*

---

[40]   Jeremiah 1:5

birds in the sky, over the livestock and all the wild animals, and over all the creatures that move along the ground."[41] He spoke in the spirit realm and told man who he was. In essence, God uploaded each of our individual identities in the spirit realm and gave us specific gifts and talents in order to fulfill each of our unique purpose in life. To that end, there are two very important questions that every individual needs to answer as they engage the process of maturity. These questions are fundamental and universal regardless of one's cultural background, socioeconomic status, country of origin, and/ or any other circumstance into which one may be born.

The Two Great Questions

The two great commandments[42] found in scripture are the foundation of our Christian faith. Likewise, the resolution of the two great questions is foundational to the maturation process that we engage throughout the course of our lives. These two great questions have everything to do with whether one lives a successful life or an unfulfilled one. The answers to these questions align with God's grand plan for each of us and we must be intentional about our exploration of, as well as, our commitment to this process of maturation at work in our lives. The first question that must be answered with clarity is, "Who am I?" The scripture says, "*My people perish because of lack of knowledge.*"[43] God is speaking to man and letting us know that if man doesn't discover the root of knowledge he will not live.

So what or who is the root of knowledge? Simply put, God is the root of knowledge. God is omniscient, meaning He is *omni* (all) *science* (the study of knowledge) or all-knowing. The message from this scripture is that man cannot live (will die) if he does not know God. If man does not know God, then he cannot and will not know himself. The bottom line is that man cannot answer the "Who am I?" question without first knowing who God is. Any man that does

---

41   Genesis 1:26
42   Matthew 22:36–40
43   Hosea 4:6

not know himself will not be able to answer or respond accurately to the second question, which is, "What is my purpose?" In order to live a successful life man must fulfill his divine purpose for life. Meaning, success in life is based on one's ability to fulfill the purpose for which he has been called. Before man can fulfill his purpose in life, he must know who he is. Prior to discovering the knowledge of one's self, one must first study to know who God is.[44] Every man must humble himself and seek the face of God in order to discover his own spiritual identity while also discerning his God-ordained, predetermined, predestined purpose in life.

A few years ago, I had a conversation with my grandmother on her 101st birthday, and she stated that there is a reason why God has kept her here so long. I could not pass up the opportunity to ask this mature woman the two questions that I believe are the most fundamental questions to every person's life. When I asked, "Grandma, who are you?" I thought I was going to get a more "her-storical" answer that was based on her life experiences. However, she simply stated, "I am a child of God!" I immediately thought about the conversation that Moses had with the Lord when he asked, "Who shall I say sent me?"[45] and the Lord responded, "I AM THAT I AM." The Holy Spirit spoke to me at that moment and said, "EVERYTHING YOU ARE BEGINS WITH I AM." I then jumped right into the second question, "Grandma, what is your purpose?" She again stated without hesitation, "To teach and impart wisdom to the young people." I got really excited because her response was aligned with the eighth hedge of the proposed maturation process (to be discussed). I took the liberty of asking another question since she was on a roll. I asked, "Grandma, what helps you to keep your perspective on life?" Grandma Annie declared, "I used to be afraid of dying and not being right but, what helps me to keep it together is forgiveness and repentance." My mature grandmother responded to these questions with confidence and a clear resolve of who she was (and is) and what her life's purpose was (and is).

---

[44] 2 Timothy 2:15
[45] Exodus 3:14

Man's identity was established from the foundation of the world and set in the spirit realm. We sat in the wisdom and counsel of God as He spoke into our spirit man and told us who we were. Another way to articulate this point is simply to say that before we were conceived in our mother's womb[46] God uploaded our identity in the spirit realm. *Identity* is defined here as the "spiritual and genetic encoding; a pre-determined role one is created to assume in the plan of God; and that which is aligned to one's life purpose." Identity is a critical piece in the process of maturity. The discovery process of one's identity begins at the child's conception into this physical world and it becomes the responsibility of the parents to train up the child according to the identity established by God in the beginning of time.[47]

The Hedges Model for Maturity

I am using the developmental theory of Erik Erikson (1968) as a backdrop for this discussion about the hedges. Erikson theorized eight stages of development and described these stages as progressive through the life cycle. During each stage of development, a person needs to develop specific relationships, resolve specific crises, and exercise specific virtues that enables the seed (or child) to develop towards maturity. If these relationships are not developed, if these crises are not resolved, and if the virtues are not experienced, then the individual experiences deficits in his or her development.[48] A brief review of the first five stages of Erikson's theory will assist with a better understanding of how identity is formed. In conjunction with Erikson's theory, I am introducing the "Hedges Model for maturity." This Hedges Model is a concept of development that identifies key covenant and committed relationships that are critical in the maturation process. Each hedge is responsible for providing the seed

---

[46]   Jeremiah 1:5: "Before I formed you in the womb I knew you, before you
         were born I set you apart; I appointed you as a prophet to the nations."
[47]   Proverbs 22:6: "Train up a child in the way he should go, And when he is old
         he will not depart from it."
[48]   Bee, 1992; Erikson, 1968; and Miller, 2002.

with, at a minimum, love, protection, encouragement, and support. When these relationships are in place, they increase the likelihood of the developing child's needs being met and the child discovering, accepting, and assuming the intended identity. These hedges are extremely important given the evil and distracting forces in this world that are working to pervert and even destroy the developing seed.[49] When these hedges are not in place, the seed is left vulnerable and exposed to the enemy's devices. It is extremely important to discuss the first four stages of development and their impact on the inner-forming (or in-formation) and outward-molding of one's identity, which usually begins to harden during the fifth stage of development.

In the first stage of development, a mother's love, protection, encouragement, support, affection, and nurturing helps to lay the foundation for an individual's trust and identity.[50] Hope is the desired virtue developed from this stage and it is crucial to the development of one's faith.[51] If the child's needs are not completely met in this stage, the child could develop a sense of hopelessness in the first eighteen months of his life. The second stage of development is when the father's presence provides another layer or hedge of love, protection, encouragement, and support (not that the father wasn't present in the first stage, yet the mother's presence[52] is so primary and profound). In the second stage, the father also provides a sense of balance between the nurturing of the mother and the structure and discipline established by the authority of the father. The child begins to learn how to self-manage, while his will is encouraged. When the father is absent, the will of the child can be damaged or even broken. The third stage of development establishes a core system of love, protection, encouragement, and support with the child's immediate

---

49   Genesis 3:15: "And I will put enmity between you and the woman, And between your seed and her Seed; He shall bruise your head, And you shall bruise His heel."

50   1 Peter 2:2: "As newborn babes, desire the pure milk of the word, that you may grow thereby..."

51   Hebrews 11:1: "Now faith is the substance of things hoped for, the evidence of things not seen."

52   Matthew 19:14: "But Jesus said, 'Let the little children come to Me, and do not forbid them; for of such is the kingdom of heaven.'"

family. Establishing the covenant relationships with one's mother, father, and siblings enables the child to develop initiative and discover a sense of purpose. When the family structure or support system is out of order, the child could develop little to no sense of direction or purpose. The fourth stage of development is when the developing child needs love, protection, encouragement, and increased support from the broader community regarding his intellectual and skill development. The African proverb that states, "It takes a village to raise a child," is appropriate for this stage. Extended family members, teachers, mentors, church members, coaches, and neighbors all have the potential to play key roles in the developing child during the fourth stage. If the child needs are not met by this stage, he can develop a sense of inferiority and feelings of incompetence.

The fifth stage which occurs during adolescence is a very pivotal stage in the developmental process. The young person should make the transition from childhood to young adulthood yet continues to need love, protection, encouragement, and support. It is during this stage that the question of identity becomes the primary crisis that needs to be resolved. The question "Who am I?" must be answered confidently by every individual. The previous four stages have a huge impact on how one's identity is formed and shaped in the fifth stage of development. This is why parents must teach and train their children in order for children to discover who God says they are. At the same time, children need to be loved, protected, encouraged, and supported at each stage in order to be in-formed and shaped as to who they are. The important relationships during this stage of development are peers, available leaders, and the most important relationship is that of the father. Children need to be affirmed by their fathers just as Jesus Christ was affirmed by God the Father when He was baptized by John the Baptist in the Jordan River.[53] As Jesus came up out of the water, God the Father declared, "This is My Beloved Son, in whom I am well-pleased." It wasn't until Christ received this affirmation from Father God that He was able to go

---

[53]   Matthew 3:17 "And suddenly a voice *came* from heaven, saying, 'This is My beloved Son, in whom I am well pleased.'"

forth and fulfill His purpose. Likewise, children need their fathers to speak into their lives and affirm their identity in our heavenly Father. The identity that was established from the beginning, and from the foundations of the world. Once affirmed, the young man develops a sense of fidelity to his spiritual identity. When the discovered identity is assumed by the individual it represents the beginning of manhood. This stage would be much like the casual son who has received salvation and has entered into fellowship with the Holy One. If the developing child has not developed the appropriate relationships and his needs have not been met, the result is very often a confusion of roles and/or an identity crisis. It is absolutely imperative for a man in the maturation process to be clear and confident about every aspect of his identity. Figure 3.1 illustrates the first stages of the "Hedges Model for Maturity."

Figure 3.1: The Hedges Model for Maturity.

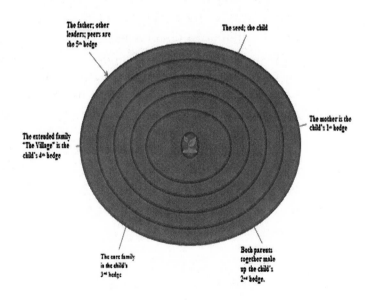

This model represents the first five hedges in the maturation process. The fundamental responsibilities in each of these relationships again are to love, to protect, to encourage, and to support. These responsibilities are carried out as the crisis and/or needs inherent within each stage of development are resolved and/or met respectively. The successful training of a child during these first five stages in the maturation process will result in the positive affirmation of a God-ordained identity. On the contrary, if a child's preparation is lacking and there are crucial relationships that are not developed, unresolved crises and/or unmet needs the child will develop deficits that often will result in an identity crisis.

During the sixth stage of development, the individual takes on greater responsibility as a young adult. Scripture reads, "When I was a child, I used to speak like a child, I thought like a child, I reasoned like a child. When I became a man, I put aside childish things."[54] Now that the young man has hopefully discovered, accepted, and assumed his identity, there is usually a need for him to seek out the love found in an intimate relationship with a woman.[55] He is looking for a helpmate as he begins to focus on and pursue his purpose in life. The young man learns to love, protect, encourage, and support himself as he also desires to love, protect, encourage, and support his wife while having her reciprocate the same toward him.[56] He embarks on a deeper study of God[57] and His holy word in order to gain a greater understanding of life and his purpose in it. Purpose is defined as "the spiritual assignment of one's life; the predetermined call on one's life." The young man in this stage of intimacy is striving for a greater level of maturity, and like the committed, son he is endeavoring to draw closer to God. It is very important to note that one must resolve the crisis of identity in the previous stage before

---

[54] 1 Corinthians 13:11
[55] Proverbs 18:22: *He who* finds a wife finds a good *thing*, and obtains favor from the LORD.
[56] Ephesians 5:25: "Husbands, love your wives, just as Christ also loved the church and gave Himself for her."
[57] Isaiah 55:6: "Seek the LORD while He may be found, Call upon Him while He is near."

attempting to pursue intimacy with someone else in this sixth stage of development. Failure to do so could lead to things such as teen pregnancy, abortion, poverty, low self-esteem, single-parent households, fatherlessness, divorce, and the dismantling of the hedges or support system that is essential for the family structure and child's development. These situations have the potential to grossly impact a child in the maturation process. When individuals come together and engage in intimate relations without having resolved the identity crisis of the previous stage it has the potential to create a situation where the child/children that result are less likely to have all of their needs met due to a lack of maturity and readiness on the part of the parents. Meaning, if parents are stuck in an identity crisis, the likelihood of their child's needs being met greatly decreases.[58] This is a dangerous and destructive cycle that needs to be broken in many families and in our society.

Once the man has been intimate with his wife, what naturally follows is the reproduction of offspring. The seventh stage of development occurs when the man becomes a father, a father figure, and/or a mentor who must learn to love, protect, encourage, support, train, and affirm his children and other youth. Genesis chapter one says, "And God blessed them, and God said unto them, be fruitful, and multiply, and replenish the earth, and subdue it: and have dominion over the fish of the sea, and over the fowl of the air, and over every living thing that moves upon the earth."[59] The man in the seventh stage begins to fulfill this scripture and he gives care to leading his family, the charge of teaching and training his children, as well as a greater focus on fulfilling his purpose in life. It is the stage when the man hones and perfects his gifts and talents as he studies to prove himself according to God's call on his life.[60] The man in this stage of generativity is experiencing the same degree of intimacy in the natural realm as the covenant son experiences in the spirit realm

---

[58]   Matthew 15:14: "And if the blind leads the blind, both will fall into a ditch."
[59]   Genesis 1:28
[60]   2 Timothy 2:15: "Be diligent to present yourself approved to God, a worker who does not need to be ashamed, rightly dividing the word of truth."

as he goes beyond the veil. If the crisis in this stage is not resolved, the results are feelings of stagnation and a lack of progress related to one's purpose.

The integrity stage of Erikson's theory focuses on the oneness that a mature man experiences when he wholly walks in the identity that God intended for him. I am defining *integrity* as "the wholeness and alignment of one's truest spiritual identity and their life's purpose within their private and public lives." The mature man has developed his God-given gifts and talents and uses them to fulfill his purpose in life. During the course of a man's life, there are many tests and trial that cause him to revert to the faith that was established in the beginning.[61] God's love enables this mature man to become the living word of God,[62] which empowers him to be an example of the Lord's love.[63] Like the covenant son, the mature man abides in God's presence and benefits from the Lord's protection.[64] The mature man is in the service of the Lord and because of his service he receives constant encouragement from the Lord.[65] The mature man receives love, support, encouragement, and support from his covenant relationships with God the Father and his fellowship within the body of Christ.[66] The man in this stage has reached the fullness of maturity. The identity that was imparted to him and the purpose for which he has been called by God is being lived out in the life of the mature man. The desire of this man is to share the wisdom that he has gleaned from the word of God and through his own life experiences. The mature man is blessed to do exceedingly and abundantly above

---

[61] Romans 5:3–5: "And not only *that,* but we also glory in tribulations, knowing that tribulation produces perseverance; and perseverance, character; and character, hope. Now hope does not disappoint, because the love of God has been poured out in our hearts by the Holy Spirit who was given to us."

[62] James 1:3–5: "Knowing that the testing of your faith produces patience. But let patience have *its* perfect work, that you may be perfect and complete, lacking nothing. If any of you lacks wisdom, let him ask of God, who gives to all liberally and without reproach, and it will be given to him."

[63] 2 Corinthians 3:2

[64] Psalms 91:1

[65] Psalms 27:14

[66] Psalms 121:2

all he could anticipate through his covenant relationship with God the Father.[67] The oneness and alignment with God's word, the man's identity, and purpose are the key aspects of this final stage. The man in this stage cannot bring unresolved crises into this stage or he will struggle with feelings of depression and despair, which can cause him to fall short of God's best for his life.

Table 3:1 – The Hedges Model for Maturity

Hedges (Love, Protection, Encouragement, & Support)	Age (Estimates)	The Crisis Love *vs.* Fear	The Important Relationship	The Need/ Virtue
1st	0 to 18 mos.	Trust *vs.* Mistrust	Mother	Hope
2nd	2 to 3 yrs.	Autonomy *vs.* Shame/Doubt	Both Parents	Will
3rd	4 to 5 yrs.	Initiative *vs.* Guilt	Core Family	Purpose
4th	6 to 12 yrs.	Industry *vs.* Inferiority	Extended Family "The Village"	Competence
5th	13 to 18 yrs.	Identity Achievement *vs.* Identity Crisis	Father, peers, and other leaders	Fidelity
6th	19 to 25 yrs.	Intimacy *vs.* Isolation	Spouse	Spousal Love
7th	26 to 39 yrs.	Generativity *vs.* Stagnation	Children and other youth	Care
8th	+40	Integrity *vs.* Despair	Oneness w/ God and His Word	Wisdom

Note. Adapted from Erikson's eight stages of psychosocial development (Erikson, 1968).

[67] Ephesians 3:20–21

Hedges of Love, Protection, Encouragement, and Support (Gen. 3:15)

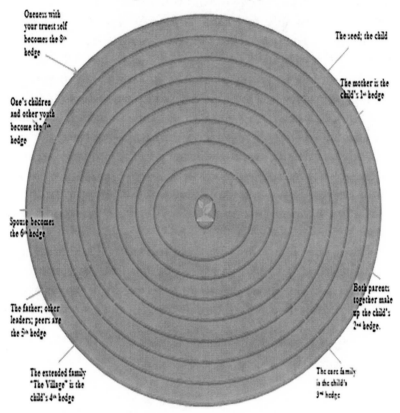

There are two great questions posed in this chapter that are fundamental to every seed born of a woman regardless of gender, ethnicity, or any other demographic category. Who am I and what is my purpose are the critical questions that every godly successful person must clearly and accurately answer. The mature man must meditate [68] on the word of God in order to discern the most appropriate responses for his life.

---

[68]   Joshua 1:8 - This book of the law shall not depart out of thy mouth; but thou shalt meditate therein day and night, that thou mayest observe to do

I challenge every man to read, study, and search the perfect law of liberty[69] for that scriptural verse that speaks specifically to you as an individual. What? Yes, I submit to you that there are specific scriptures that speak directly to who you are and what your purpose is. Here is an example. My name is John W. Hatcher III, and the scripture that speaks to who I am and what my purpose is comes from 3 John:2.[70] The scripture states, "Beloved, I wish above all things that thou may prosper in all things and be in health, just as your soul prospers." It starts with the "Beloved" and John means the beloved of God or God's grace. I am the III John and the second born son. I am a licensed teacher of health, and God has given me the concept of wellness to minister health and healing to the body of Christ. The concept of wellness is about living in an even or balanced way in the physical, mental, social, emotional, economical, and spiritual aspects of life. What scripture speaks to you? Where are you found in the scriptures?

Thank you, Father, for Your grace and mercy! I ask, in the name of Jesus, that you lay upon the hearts of Your men servants to first know who You are; so we can know who we are as we engage the Great Commission according to Your will for our lives individually and collectively, in Jesus's name I pray. Amen!

---

according to all that is written therein: for then thou shalt make thy way prosperous, and then thou shalt have good success.

[69] James 1:25 - But whoso looketh into the perfect law of liberty, and continueth therein, he being not a forgetful hearer, but a doer of the work, this man shall be blessed in his deed.

[70] 3 John:2 - Beloved, I wish above all things that you mayest prosper and be in health, even as thy soul prospereth.

CHAPTER 4

How Does Man Live a Balanced Life?

*Beloved, I wish above all things that you would prosper
and be in health,* even *as your soul prospers.*[71]

Wellness, Wholeness, and Holiness

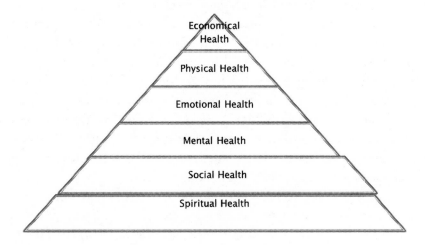

- Economical Health
- Physical Health
- Emotional Health
- Mental Health
- Social Health
- Spiritual Health

---

[71]   3 John:2

An Introduction to Wellness, Wholeness, and Holiness

Wellness, wholeness, and *holiness* are three terms that are used in a variety of circumstances; however, when they are examined closely they can, in many instances, be synonymous with one another. At the heart of these terms are the core ideas of completeness, fullness, totality, and unity in life and alignment with the *truth* of God's word. I previously shared that the book of 3 John verse number 2 is who I am in the context of scripture. I believe that this scripture is the essence of my identity and purpose in Christ Jesus. I am the beloved of God, God's grace, and my wife calls me Love, which also speaks to the essence of who I am. First John 4:8[72] reminds us that God is *love*. I am absolutely not saying that I am God (*love*), nor am I my wife's god. However, I am saying that I am (love) because that is who I have been called by my Heavenly Father to be. I am the beloved of God! I am made in the image of my Father, and I am a licensed teacher of health and physical education. I began receiving revelation on the concept of wellness by studying the word of God and by applying myself to the art and science of teaching and learning health concepts. I am defining *wellness* as "the highest level of health one can achieve to include each of the six aspects of health." Interestingly, the number six is considered the number of man. The six aspects of man's health are physical health, mental health, social health, emotional health, economic health, and spiritual health. Wellness[73] is a concept that promotes balanced and holistic living through these six aspects of life and it represents successful living. *Health* is defined as "the quality of life that relates to one's body, mind, relationships, feelings, finances, soul, and spirit." One must give the necessary time and attention to each facet of health in order to aspire to wellness.

Contrary to each of the six aspects of health there are corresponding illnesses associated respectively. *Every* illness *represents a disorder, a disfunction, a disease, and or a disruption as it relates to*

---

[72] 1 John 4:8: "Whoever does not love does not know God, because God is love."

[73] Matthew 6:33: "But seek ye first the kingdom of God, and his righteousness; and all these things shall be added unto you."

any or all aspects of health. Examples of physical illnesses that have an impact on the body are conditions such as cancer, heart disease, and the common cold. Examples of illnesses related to mental health that affect the mind include but are not limited to, learning disabilities, dyslexia, neurodevelopmental disorder, and bipolar disorders. Examples of social illnesses that impact relationships include poor communication skills, fatherlessness, bad manners, and disrespect. Emotional illnesses are things such as uncontrolled anger, low self-esteem, schizophrenia, and depression. When it comes to economical illnesses we look at things such as poverty, unemployment, poor money management, and bad credit. Finally, spiritual illnesses include a lack of the knowledge of God, double-mindedness, disobedience, and basically sin of all types. The reason that there are illnesses in each aspect of health is that every aspect of one's being has a divine order, function, flow, and purpose. When the prescribed order, function, flow, and purpose of one's being is not achieved it leads toward death. Until a man has been healed from every manner of dis-ease, until he has been strengthened in each aspect of health, and until he can maintain a high quality of life in each and every aspect of health he has not achieved a wellness status.

An Overview of the Six Aspects of Health

The concept of wellness represents six parts of a man's life that must be given the necessary attention in a balanced way. This discussion will highlight some relevant components of each aspect of health and it also alludes to a plan for improving and maintaining one's personal health status. Using this chapter, each reader will have the opportunity to develop their own Personal Wellness Plan (see appendix A). The Personal Wellness Plan (PWP) assignment is designed to assist each individual with developing goals for each of the six aspects of health that are tethered to scripture.

The story of Samson in the Book of Judges illustrates the life of a mighty man who struggled to find a sense of balance in all six aspects of his life. Samson was a mighty man physically, mentally, economically, and spiritually. However, socially and emotionally he was found wanting and that fact led to his demise. Samson's physical and spiritual strength is told of in his great exploits facing a lion and bear, as well as, the slaying of a thousand Philistines with the jawbone of an ass.[74] Economically, his family had resources enough to provide him with the wife he desired. Samson's mental capacity is evidenced in the fact that he was a judge in Israel for at least twenty years. Although Samson's quality of life was (at least) good in three aspects of his life and superior physically, he died with his eyes having been plucked out because socially and emotionally he experienced deficits. If that great and mighty man Samson would have gotten some assistance with addressing his social and emotional issues how much greater could he have been. How much greater would you be if you were made whole in each of the six aspects of life?

The first aspect of health to be discussed is without question the most important aspect of health; however, many times it gets the least amount of attention. Spiritual health is the aspect of health that relates to one's soul and spirit. Some key elements of spiritual health that are mentioned here are studying the word of God, prayer and fasting, faith, and the sharing of the Gospel of Jesus Christ. *Studying the Word of God* is a key element in the discovery of spiritual identity and the pursuit of one's life purpose. Studying the word of God,[75] as well as studying the specific area of discipline related to your calling within the context of the word of God is paramount for the mature man. Studying is crucial to acquiring knowledge, to getting understanding, and to gaining wisdom of a specific subject matter (www.studygs. net). Studying enables the mature individual to love and worship the Lord with his mind. The next component of spiritual health that should be explored is prayer. *Prayer* is communication with God.[76] In order for men to develop intimacy with God they must pray. Jesus Christ gives instruction on how a mature individual should pray.[77] Using scripture to pray in faith demonstrates one's agreement with

---

[74]   The Book of Judges
[75]   Study the Word of God—Luke 10:27 and 2 Timothy 2:15
[76]   Prayer—Matthew 6:9-13, Luke 18:1, 1 Thessalonians 5:17
[77]   Matthew 6:9–13

God's word and guarantees a favorable outcome for the mature man. *Fasting* is a component of spiritual health that involves abstaining from some food and/or drink or some fleshly desire or need for religious observance (www.sentara.com). The purpose of fasting is at least twofold, in that, it allows time for the cleansing of the body and rejuvenation of the digestive tract.[78] Fasting also enables the spirit man time to be fed and strengthened in order to keep the natural (fleshly) man in check. This twofold purpose allows the mature man to focus on who he is and to use his time and resources on fulfillment of purpose. The final element of spiritual health is *ministry*, which is the *opportunity to meet the needs of people while sharing the gospel of Jesus Christ.*[79] The mature man is constantly in the mode of ministry whether it is in his role as a husband, a father, a leader, or as a mentor.

The second aspect of health to be explored briefly is social health, which focuses on relationships. The key components of social health shared here are communication, cooperation, conflict resolution, and manners. *Communication*[80] is an important part of any relationship and is necessary for all relationships to progress toward intimacy. Engaging in effective communication requires the mature man to express his thoughts, feelings, and ideas, as well as listening to and accurately interpreting the thoughts, feelings, and ideas of others. The three parts of communication include a sender, a message, and a receiver (www.dalecarnegie.com). One must assess their ability to effectively communicate in a variety of relationship types. *Cooperation* can be defined simply as mutual effort with regard to a common objective (www.thesaurus.com). The saying, "No man is an island unto himself"[81] suggests that all men, at some point, need to connect with others in order to accomplish some objective. A mature man understands that cooperation is an important component of social health. Likewise, conflict resolution is an important component of social heath necessary for maintaining healthy relationships. *Conflict*

---

78   Fasting—Matthew 17:21 and Isaiah 58
79   Ministry—Matthew 28:19 and 20
80   Communication—1 Thessalonians 5:17
81   Cooperation—Matthew 18:20

resolution is a process of mediating problems in a relationship that ensures the relationship remains the priority as pressures build (www. mindtools.com). As personal relationships develop, conflicts[82] will surface which provide opportunities to maintain and strengthen these relationships. *Manners* are the final component of social health to be mentioned in this section. In our daily interactions with other people there are some minimal expectations for a mature individual.[83] The mature man has a basic respect for all people in a diverse and ever-changing society (www.emilypost.com).

Mental health is the third aspect of health to be considered with regard to the "Where are you?" question. Mental health refers to the quality and state of one's mind. When we began to understand the words and the instruction of Christ, then we are developing towards mental maturity. Mental maturity is demonstrated through the transformation of our carnal minds into alignment with the spiritual mind of Christ. The key components of mental health mentioned here are learning, meditation, critical thinking, and strategic planning.

Evaluating one's level of learning is crucial to assessing the maturity of one's mind. *Learning* is a process of engaging a body of knowledge that leads to mastery of that same body of knowledge.[84] There are six levels of learning that one experiences as he progresses toward maturity within a discipline (www.successcenter.truman. edu). *Meditation* can be defined as a deliberate process of reflecting and focusing on a single topic.[85] Meditation facilitates deeper levels of learning and promotes mastery of the subject matter, which leads to successful use of the acquired knowledge.

Critical thinking is a key component of mental health that demonstrates the mental maturity one must possess in order to engage high levels of intellectual processes.[86] The Critical Thinking Foundation defines *critical thinking* as, "the intellectually disciplined process of actively and skillfully conceptualizing,

---

[82] Conflict Resolution—Matt. 18:15–17
[83] Manners—Matt. 7:12
[84] Learning—2 Timothy 2:15
[85] Meditation—Joshua 1:8
[86] Critical Thinking—Eccl. 12:13

applying, analyzing, synthesizing, and/or evaluating information gathered from, or generated by, observation, experience, reflection, reasoning, or communication, as a guide to belief and action" (www. criticalthinking.org). The mature man is a critical thinker, as well as, a strategic planner. *Strategic planning* is a part of mental health processes that involves planning and developing steps to accomplish a goal.[87] The purpose of strategic planning is to focus efforts and maximize resources in order to fulfill a vision. Like playing the game of chess, the mature man must participate in strategic planning in order to fulfill his purpose in life.

The fourth aspect of health reviewed briefly in regard to the "Where are you?" question is emotional health which is related to one's feelings. The key components of emotional health that will be quickly assessed here are love, fear, excitement, and anger. *Love*[88] is the first and most important component of emotional health. Love is also the most important component of overall personal wellness and expands throughout all aspects of health. That means that, love can be expressed physically, mentally, socially, emotionally, economically, and spiritually. The mature man understands how to appropriately express his love in a variety of relationships to include; his relationship with God, his family, and within his community. *Fear*[89] is the next component assessed in regard to emotional health and it is contrary to love. Fear is an emotion that causes one to feel threatened or in danger (www.humanillness.com). Remember, Adam separated himself from God because of fear. The mature man is not timid but, he is strong, loving, courageous and self-disciplined. The only fear that supports one in pursuit of purpose is the fear God. *Excitement* is another component of emotional health that is helpful when fulfilling purpose. When a man has matured to the point of knowing his spiritual identity, he has invested time into developing his gifts and talents, and he is striving to fulfill his purpose in life

---

[87]   Strategic planning—Habakkuk 2:2 and Luke 14:28
[88]   Love—1 John 4:8, Matthew 22:37–39, and 1 Corinthians 13:1–13
[89]   Fear—2 Timothy 1:7; The fear of God—Psalm 115:11

there is an excitement[90] that is unmatched when it comes to his work. The mature man that has discovered his calling is motivated to do the work required to fulfill his call even if he doesn't get paid for it. The mature man might live according to the motto that says, "Lord give me life until my work is done and give me work until my life shall end." The final component of emotional health is anger. Anger[91] is a strong feeling of displeasure or hostility (www.thefreedictionary.com). *Anger* is a very dangerous emotion because it can cause one to bypass rational thought processes and the use of good judgment. The mature man manages his anger in a way that addresses the source of displeasure without sinning against God. The mature man is very aware of his feelings and he does well to manage them accordingly.

Physical health is the fifth aspect of health to be addressed with respect to the question "Where are you?" Physical health is the quality of life related to the condition of one's body. The word of God informs us that our bodies are the temple of the Holy Spirit,[92] which simply means that we must prepare ourselves for the spirit of God to dwell in us. Physical maturity is a physiological process that naturally occurs over time as the systems of the body complete their developmental processes. Every cell in the body has a divine order according to its creative design. The whole body is fitly joined, which is emblematic of the body of Christ.[93] Like cells in our own body have a specific place and a specific function, so it is, that we have a specific place and specific function in the body of Christ. [94]We must present our bodies as living sacrifices holy and acceptable unto God and this is our reasonable service. There are some important things we must pay attention to when preparing ourselves for the master's use. We will explore four key components that have the potential to greatly impact one's physical health status. The four components are nutritional status, fitness level, rest, and hygiene.

---

[90]   Excitement—Psalm 69:9
[91]   Anger—Ecclesiastes 7:9
[92]   1 Corinthians 6:19 and 20
[93]   Ephesians 4:16
[94]   Romans 12:1

Exploring one's *nutritional status* requires that the individual would consider their recommended daily allowance for food intake, as well as their dietary history (Maqbool, Olsen, and Stallings, 2008). Nutritional status is extremely important when assessing overall physical health.[95] As the saying goes, "You are what you eat!" So, if you eat GMOs (genetically modified organisms), then you should expect the effects of that action to manifest itself in the health status of your body. Another very important component of physical health is an individual's *fitness level.* Assessing fitness level provides the individual with the necessary information about their body's efficiency and performance (www.adultfitness.org). The US Centers for Disease Control and Prevention encourages the adult public, ages eighteen to sixty-four, to engage each week in at least one and a quarter hours of vigorous-intensity aerobic activity or two and a half hours of moderate-intensity aerobic activity; that time can be met in any increments. The daily performance and work requires one to rest and rejuvenate the body.[96] *Rest* is essential to the continuous healing process of the body.[97] The Mayo Clinic suggests seven to eight hours of rest for adults (www.sleepfoundation.org). Rest is so important to the maintenance of good health that God built in one whole day of the week solely for its purpose. The final component used here to assess overall physical health is *hygiene.*[98] *Merriam-Webster* online defines hygiene as "the condition or practice (as of cleanliness) conducive to health" (www.meriam-webster.com). The purpose of hygiene primarily is to rid the body of germs and other disease causing agents for the body and like repentance, forgiveness, and the blood of Jesus will free the soul from sin. These four components of physical health can be used to explore the mature man's health status giving consideration for his age.

The sixth aspect of health to be examined briefly is economic health, which relates to one's finances. *Employment*[99] status is a critical

---

[95]   Nutritional Status - I Corinthians 10:31
[96]   Fitness level—Philippians 2:12
[97]   Rest—Exodus 23:12
[98]   Hygiene—1 Thessalonians 5:23
[99]   Employment—Genesis 3:19 and 2 Thessalonians 3:10

factor of economic health and involves earning a wage or salary as a result of a work effort. Having an income source is a priority for the mature man and his responsibility in support of himself and his family. Focused resources are necessary when one is in pursuit of purpose (www.fulfilling-life-purpose.com). *Tithes and taxes*[100] are two additional components of economic health. *Tithe* is that first 10 percent of your earnings that goes toward the up-building of God's kingdom. The mature man allocates his resources in a manner that supports kingdom building. Taxes are that portion of one's earnings that goes to the government (www.irs.gov). Christ said render unto Caesar that which belongs to Caesar and unto God that which belongs to God.

Investment[101] is another component of economic health that is important to financial stewardship. It is important for an individual to work toward fulfillment of purpose and it is equally important for one to ensure his resources are working for him (www.daveramsey. com). The parable of the talents expressly illustrates the concept of investment in that a portion was given and an increase on the return was expected. *Credit* is a component of one's financial stewardship that is rated based on the US financial system's confidence in an individual's likelihood to pay his debts (www.consumercredit.com). A mature man uses wisdom and discretion as to how he uses his credit.[102] These four components of finance help to identify what is considered good stewardship.

As I continued to study the concept of wellness I began to understand more and more that it is a way to live a completely balanced and successful life.[103] I eventually came to understand wellness as being synonymous with the ideals of wholeness[104] and holiness.[105]

---

[100]   Tithes and Taxes—Malachi 3:8, Matthew 22:21, and Luke 20:25
[101]   Investment—Ecclesiastes 11:1 and Galatians 6:7
[102]   Proverbs 22:7
[103]   Joshua 1:8: "Keep this Book of the Law always on your lips; meditate on it day and night, so that you may be careful to do everything written in it. Then you will be prosperous and successful."
[104]   John 5:14: "Afterward Jesus findeth him in the temple, and said unto him, Behold, thou art made whole."
[105]   Hebrews 12:14: "Follow peace with all men, and holiness, without which no man shall see the Lord."

The integrity and maturity with which all of us should aspire to and live out in our daily lives has everything to do with developing our body, our mind, our relationships, managing and subduing our passions, being a good financial steward, and allowing our soul and spirit to align with the word of the Lord Jesus. Furthermore, as we achieve a high quality of life in each aspect of our lives, we must then focus on maintaining good health. Maintaining a good health status in each of the six aspects of living while balancing efforts in every aspect will lead to overall wellness.

Wholeness and holiness, like wellness, are the results of following divine instructions on how to live and develop toward maturity. I have defined *wholeness* as "the sum of one; not lacking any parts; complete and together; fitly joined; representing a state of complex unity." The eighth stage in the development or maturation process (Hedges Model) discussed in chapter 3 represents integrity and wholeness. When you think of the seed that develops through each stage of life and receives the love, protection, encouragement, and support from the key relationships while also resolving the corresponding conflicts associated with each stage, the results are wholeness and integrity in life. The mature man will experience and share in the wisdom produced through this state of integrity and wholeness. So I will repeat the question that Jesus asked, "Will you be made whole (man)?"

A life of holiness is a loving response to a loving and holy God.
—Bishop Carlton McCleod

In the context of this work I have defined *holiness* as "a lifestyle by which one lives in strict obedience to God's word and His commandments and ordinances." The decision to strictly adhere to God's commandments and ordinances is the essence of holiness. One can be assured of living well when dedicated to a life of holiness. The word of our Lord gives clear and specific instructions that speak directly to how we should live physically, mentally, socially, emotionally, economically, and spiritually. The Bible informs man how to develop, strengthen, maintain, and even heal the body, mind, relationships, feelings, finances, and the soul. If a man adheres to the instructions found in the holy scriptures, then he would be considered living a life of holiness.

The following scriptural references are a few examples of how Bible verses relate to wellness and holiness. In his first letter to the church at Corinth, the Apostle Paul presented this instruction, "*Do you not know that your bodies are members of Christ himself? Do you not know that he who unites himself with a prostitute is one with her in body? For it is said, the two will become one flesh. But whoever is united with the Lord is one with him in spirit. Flee from sexual immorality. All other sins a person commits are outside the body, but whoever sins sexually, sins against their own body. Do you not know that your bodies are temples of the Holy Spirit, who is in you, whom you have received from God? You are not your own...*"[106] Paul gives sound instruction to man here on how to govern the body in holiness as a dwelling place for our God.

The beauty of holiness extends to the mind when a man rethinks the patterns of his thoughts and he submits to the holy mind of God. *Do not conform to the pattern of this world, but be transformed by the renewing of your mind. Then you will be able to test and approve what God's will is—His good, pleasing, and perfect will.*[107] When a mature man's mind aligns with the will and the word of God he is fulfilling that portion of the first great commandment to love our heavenly Father wholly and completely. A lifestyle of holiness is also played out in man's relationship with God, himself, and his neighbor. Christ while being tested was asked, "*Teacher, which is the greatest commandment in the law. Jesus replied, love the Lord your God with all your heart, and with all your soul, and with all your mind. This is the first and greatest commandment. The second is like it, love your neighbor as yourself. All the law and the prophets hang on these two commandments.*"[108] A man who understands how to love God with his whole heart, soul, and mind and is doing so is on the path of

---

[106] Holiness—1 Corinthians 6:15–19 (body)
[107] Romans 12:2 (mind)
[108] Matthew 22:36–40 (relationships)

holiness. In addition, this mature man demonstrates love for himself by living out his divine identity and purpose while encouraging and supporting others to do the same.

Moreover, a man's feelings, finances, and his soul are likewise governed by the holy scriptures. James, the brother of Christ, instructs the body of believers in this manner, "*My dear brothers and sisters, take note of this: Everyone should be quick to listen, slow to speak and slow to become angry…*"[109] This sound teaching empowers the mature man in the management of his feelings and gives clear direction for living holy. The scriptures declare that the love of money is the root of evil; while the old testament prophet poses the question, "*Will a man rob God?*"[110] He continues, "*Yet you are robbing Me! But you say, 'How have we robbed You?' In tithes and offerings.*" The decision to pay tithes and give an offering are indeed acts of worship and they furthermore demonstrate the path of holiness in the area of a mature man's finances. This holds true because it is always easy to discern where a man's heart is by where and how he directs his money. Finally, holiness is lived out through obedience to God's word and with the integrity of the Holy Spirit of God. The Bible declares, "*God is spirit, and his worshipers must worship in the Spirit and in truth.*"[111] Loving our God, serving our God, and worshiping our God in the beauty of holiness is, "a loving response to a loving and holy God!"

So, man of God "will you *be* made whole?"[112] Will you *be* perfect as our Father in heaven is perfect?[113] Will you *be* holy as our Father in heaven is Holy?[114] In the end we must, "*Follow peace with all men*, understanding that…*holiness, without which no man shall see the Lord.*" Yet, the mature man wants to hear our Lord say, "Well done, you good and faithful servant…"[115] Let us do well to live this balanced lifestyle while giving the necessary time and attention to

---

[109] James 1:19 (feelings)
[110] Malachi 3:8–10 (finances)
[111] John 4:24 (soul and spirit)
[112] John 5:6
[113] Matthew 5:48
[114] 1 Peter 1:16
[115] Matthew 25:23

each aspect of our health and always striving to align our day-to-day living with God's word!

Father God, in the name of Jesus, we pray that You would encourage the hearts of every person that reads this book to study Your word and to understand Your instructions for life. Help us Lord to not just be hearers of Your word but doers also. Encourage us where we are strong and heal us in our areas of weakness, so that we will be made whole in You! In the matchless name of Jesus we pray! Amen!

CHAPTER 5

What Are the Duties of Man?

And Jesus came and spoke to them, saying, "All authority has been given to Me in heaven and on earth. Go therefore and make disciples of all the nations, baptizing them in the name of the Father and of the Son and of the Holy Spirit, teaching them to observe all things that I have commanded you; and lo, I am with you always, even to the end of the age." Amen.[116]

The Worker, the Warrior, and the Worshiper

---
[116]   Matthew 28:18–20

What are the duties of man?[117]

In response to the question, what are the duties of man, I have taken the liberty of using images of eagles to represent what I am calling WWW. This is not the commonly used beginnings of a website address; however, *WWW* represents the three duties of a man to be discussed in this chapter. God has charged every man to work,[118] to war,[119] and to worship.[120] The mature man has a strong work ethic, he knows how to fight and with whom he is fighting (who or what he is fighting for and who or what he is fighting against), and the mature man understands the awesomeness of submitting to a holy God in the act of worship. Every man needs to work! Every man needs to war! Every man needs to worship! We are going to explore these three duties of a man; however, I want to reference a scripture shared previously found in the book of [121]Job 38:3[122] that admonishes you to brace yourself. There is no side stepping these questions, there is no getting around them, you have got to respond to some very important questions. You don't have to answer them for me, but you do need to answer these questions.

The overarching question is "Where are you, man?"; however, some additional and relevant questions also demand your response. Where are you in your relationship with God? Where are you as it relates to the work and purpose for which you have been called? Where are you in regard to being a hedge of protection for your heart, your family, and your community from the devil's devices? Where are you when it comes to engaging the call of God on your

---

[117]   Eccl. 12:13: "Let us hear the conclusion of the whole matter: Fear God, and keep his commandments: for this *is* the whole *duty* of man."

[118]   Genesis 3:19: "By the sweat of your brow you will eat your food until you return to the ground."

[119]   Ephesians 6:10–13: "Finally, my brethren, be strong in the Lord and in the power of His might. Put on the whole armor of God, that you may be able to stand against the wiles of the devil."

[120]   John 4:23; "Yet a time is coming and has now come when the true worshipers will worship the Father in the Spirit and in truth, for they are the kind of worshipers the Father seeks."

[121]   Brace yourself like a man; I will question you, and you shall answer me.

[122]   Brace yourself like a man; I will question you, and you shall answer me.

life? As you draw closer to God, the image of you and the plans that He has for your life will become more and more clear. So, are you a mature man? I'm asking these questions, but it is not about your immediate response. It is about every man examining himself, so these are questions you need to ponder in your meditation with the Lord.

Another question is related to a term I have overheard some young people use with regard to the amount of effort they exhibit in a variety of activities. The question is, do you go hard; which means are you maximizing your efforts. The follow-up question would be, what are you going hard after? It is one thing to go hard after women, money, or even some form of power to demonstrate your masculinity. However, are you going hard after the things of God? Are you going hard after those things which are eternal? Are you going hard after those things that honor and bring glory to the Lord Jesus? Do you understand what you are going hard after? As a mature man, are you going hard? I want you to think about this question, ponder this question in terms of the worker, the warrior, and the worshiper.

The Worker –

As we stated previously in chapter 1, man received the consequence of having to work by the sweat of his brow for his sin of disobedience. Man is to work until he returned to the ground from which he came. The *worker* is "one who labors for a cause; a person who extends the necessary efforts toward accomplishing a task." "*I must work the works of Him who sent me while it is day; the night is coming when no man can work.*"[123] A reasonable interpretation of this verse could be that, a man should labor in the area of his calling while he is young and has strength, because old age is coming and the opportunity to work will decrease. You will notice in the picture of the eagle that the eagle is at work fishing for its food. The eagle's wings are stretched wide as it has swooped down to catch a fish for a meal.[124] The picture of the eagle fishing embodies the idea of the worker. Men, we have to work![125]

So we have to be workers physically, we have to be workers mentally, we have to be workers socially, emotionally, economically, and spiritually. We work physically as we learn to exercise our bodies. That is apart of maintaining the strength of your temple. Keeping your body fit, you have to learn to work it out. The scripture says work out your soul salvation with fear and trembling; which means to align and adjust your life to the word of God. You study to show yourself approved[126] so that you can rightly divide the word of truth. That is working out mentally. A social work out occurs when your brother offends you. The scripture says, go to him one on one, and then if he doesn't receive you, then you go before the elders. So you are working out this relationship using conflict resolution. If there is a kink in the flow of your finances, you might need to get a job or set a budget for your spending. There are ways to work out physically, mentally, socially, emotionally, economically, and spiritually. There are ways we have to work out in each aspect of health. Likewise, we have to learn to war in each aspect of health.

---

[123] John 9:4: "I must work the works of him that sent me, while it is day: the night cometh, when no man can work."

[124] Thessalonians 3:10: "For even when we were with you, we gave you this rule: 'If a man will not work, he shall not eat.'"

[125] 1 Timothy 5:8: "But if any provide not for his own, and especially for those of his own house, he hath denied the faith, and is worse than an infidel."

[126] 2 Timothy 2:15

The great commission[127] charges us to go ye therefore and teach all nations, that is the co-mission. It is our mission in partnership with the Lord! We are partnering with the Lord to go into all the nations baptizing in the name of the Father, the Son, and of the Holy Ghost and we are doing it as coworkers or co-missionaries cooperating with Jesus. As ministers, we are co-missioned to do the work that we are assigned as mature men. We have all been commissioned as mature men to take up our crosses and do the work…let us put our hands to the gospel and not turn back because every man has to work!

The Warrior

One of the basic responsibilities of a man is to provide protection for those he is in relationship with. Every man should realize that we have a real enemy who comes to steal, kill, and destroy and that we must learn to war in the spirit realm. The *warrior* is "the one who fights for and protects everyone and everything given to his charge." The scripture says, *"Finally, be strong in the Lord and in his mighty power. Put on the full armor of God, so that you can take your stand against the devil's schemes. For our struggle is not against flesh and blood, but against the rulers, against the authorities, against the powers of this dark world and against the spiritual forces of evil in the heavenly realms. Therefore, put on the full armor of God, so that when*

---

[127]   Mathew 28:18–20

the day of evil comes, you may be able to stand your ground, and after you have done everything, to stand.[128] This scripture admonishes the mature man to stand in opposition of Satan's devices. It identifies that the war is not in the physical realm but, in the spiritual realm. The scripture further encourages that we equip ourselves to resist the devil when the time comes. The image of the eagle representing the warrior symbolizes a soldier protecting his country. The eagle is standing at attention and it is on guard watching out for the enemy. The warrior is looking around; he's watching and he got that look that we'll call the "eagle's eye." He's ready for warfare. He's ready to go against anyone and anything that would come against him. The duty to protect is a responsibility that every man has in each aspect of health. If someone threatened to do physical harm to my family, it is a reasonable expectation that the necessary force would be used to eliminate that threat.[129] I have to go to war to protect my family, that is part of my responsibility. Mentally, I am thinking of a chessboard. If you are familiar with how to play chess, then you understand that mentally you are going to war. It is a game of strategy where you are putting your mind, your strategic thinking against someone else's. You are working it out and you are engaging warfare. I submit to you that chess is about life. In that, there is a king in all of us. That is the King of kings, King Jesus! And there are forces that are coming after our king. We have to use and be used as we position ourselves around people who will protect us and support us as we do the same for them. We have got to learn how to war mentally. The mature man must protect his family financially by being employed, engaged in business, and create multiple streams of income, while also having various types of insurance. I'm married with five children; if something were to happen to me, I need to make sure that they are protected financially. If I was to be called home by the Lord they should not be homeless within six month. I have that responsibility as a man to guard them, to protect

---

[128] Ephesians 6:10–13
[129] Matthew 11:12: "And from the days of John the Baptist until now the kingdom of heaven suffereth violence, and the violent take it by force."

them financially. I love my wife and we've been married for more than twenty two years now. One of the questions that I love for her to ask me is, "Are you guarding my heart? Are you protecting us?" What she's asking is are you protecting our marriage. I protect our marriage by being careful of what say and see. Also, by not allowing inappropriate things to be said or done that will allow inappropriate things to creep in. Am I guarding our relationship? So we have to be protectors in every aspect again, physically, mentally, socially, emotionally, economically, and spiritually. Spiritually,[130] the weapons of our warfare are not carnal but mighty through God. We need to use the proverbs and instruction found in scripture to protect ourselves, our families, and those in our communities. How many of you are married? How many of you that are married would die for your wife? I believe I would. But how many of us die to self when we come in conflict with our wives? We say we would die, lay down our lives as Christ did for the church, which is absolutely correct. We would die for our wives, give up our lives, but when it comes to denying ourselves or even submitting ourselves when there is a conflict, do we die to self or the inner-me? It is just a question, but I want you to think about it. We have to learn to protect our families even from ourselves and that beast called pride. We have to know how to war. Do we have our armor on? Are we prepared to fight these generational curses? In this spiritual warfare, we have to become the priest, the spiritual leaders in our home. Are we prepared to call on our heavenly Father to dispatch angels into our home to protect and keep our families. To protect them while they are in school or at work. Do we pray…Lord please establish a hedge of protection around my family as they travel to and from their several destinations. There are forces that are coming against them all the time, and guess what, they're trying to attach to them when they come home. Are we discerning enough to engage spiritual warfare, to pray, to resist every spirit that is contrary to the word of God? Are we ready for war? Because every man must war!

---

[130] 2 Corinthians 10:4: "For the weapons of our warfare are not carnal, but mighty through God to the pulling down of strong holds."

The Worshiper

My pastor Bishop Carlton McCleod often shares that "worship is a loving response to a loving God." I would like to add that worshipping the Lord with all our heart, with all our mind, with all our soul, and with all our strength is an intentional act of a mature man. The *worshiper* is a "spiritually mature covenant Son of God; one who experiences God in spirit and in truth with every spiritual sense" (i.e., hearing, taste, sight, smell, and touch).

God is a Spirit: and they that worship Him must worship Him in spirit and in truth.[131] Since God is a spirit, those of us who wish to truly reverence Him should understand that it is a requisite to do so in the spirit of holiness and according to the words of truth. The image of the eagle in this section is worshiping as its wings are fully extended. Unlike the eagle whose wings are at work when the eagle flies low, the eagle who is soaring at a very high altitude is carried by the winds. The worshiping eagle is at such a great height that it only has to stretch out its wings and the wind beneath him bears him up.[132] I submit to you that just as the Lord told me years ago to "fly,

---

[131]   John 4:24: "God *is* a Spirit: and they that worship him must worship *him* in spirit and in truth."

[132]   Isaiah 40:31: "But they who wait for the Lord shall renew their strength; they shall mount up with wings like eagles; they shall run and not be weary; they shall walk and not faint."

eagle, fly." There is a point in our praise and worship when we draw closer to the Lord and our praise transitions into worship. Using the analogy of the eagle, I believe the Lord doesn't just want us to "fly, eagle, fly," but He desires that we would "soar eagle soar." The eagle's wings (in worship mode) are stretched out and are no longer at work. He doesn't have to flap his wings now because the wind carries him. He's at an altitude where he can just stretch out as the winds move him through a very high place, he's in a place of worship and this is where the Lord wants us to be with him. When we are close to him we can just lay prostrate before Him. It is not about our works, we just have to stretch out in faith and the Holy Spirit of God will carry us and lead us. This is where He wants us to be. "Draw close to Me and I'll draw close to you," says the Lord.[133]

There are two types of people that I would like to discuss and compare them with two different birds. There are eagles and there are chickens. One bird can soar high above the clouds, while the other can barely and does rarely leave the ground. Why is this important? This is significant because the storms of life will come and the chicken, who can't fly, has to endure and be concerned with every challenge that each storm will bring. The eagle, on the other hand will swing low only to get a meal and will return to higher heights. When the storms of life come the eagle has the ability to fly above the storm, so even though the storms of life may be raging, there is a place in worship where we can rise above the storm as we draw nearer to our Heavenly Father. *He who dwells in the secret place of the Most High shall abide under the shadows of the Almighty.*[134] There is a place that God desires us to be in worship. The worker is important, the warrior is necessary, yet what is most essential is the act of worship. Friends, I submit to you that many times this is what we give the least attention to and it is what's needed most. You can lie your body prostrate before the Lord in worship. You can lead your family in worship, you can worship in your giving, you can even worship in

---

133 James 4:8: "Draw near to God and He will draw near to you."
134 Psalms 91:1: "He that dwells in the secret place of the Most High shall abide under the shadow of the Almighty."

your studies. Did you know that when you read, when you study God's word, when you pray and God begins to speak to you and reveal Himself to you there is a level of worship in your study that takes place in your mind? He said love the Lord with all your heart, with all your soul, with all your mind, that is saying He wants you to worship Him holistically.[135] God expects us to worship Him with all our mind, worship with all our heart, with all our soul, and with all of our strength. Worship the Lord wholly, meaning completely. The mature man must demonstrate his responsibility to meeting the expectation ascribed to each of these duties.[136]

You shall mount up with wings like eagles, fly eagle fly! Write a reflection examining yourself as a worker, a warrior, and a worshiper in the context of the physical, mental, social, emotional, economical, and spiritual aspects of your life.[137] Now, I challenge you to have a discussion with someone you believe to be a mature man about the duties of a man: about the worker; about the warrior; and about the worshiper. Have that conversation with a mature man (or group of mature men) and then I challenge you to have a conversation with someone that you are mentoring about the worker, the warrior, and the worshiper.

What new understandings did you get from your conversations and/or what were your takeaways?

_____

_____

_____

_____

_____

_____

_____

_____

---

135   Mark 12:30: "Love the Lord your God with all your heart and with all your soul and with all your mind and with all your strength."
136   Galatians 6:5: "For every man shall bear his own burden."
137   Isaiah 40:31

CHAPTER 6

The Husband, the Father, the Leader, and the Mentor

My covenant brother and pastor Bishop Carlton McCleod, senior pastor of Calvary Revival Church of Chesapeake Virginia, shared the following passage as he communicated his vision for the church:

> Imagine a person, totally in love with Christ and passionately grateful for His sacrifice at Calvary, which

redeemed them from sin. Imagine the priority in this person's life to "self-govern" according to Scripture… to line up every part of their life according to the precepts, principles, and patterns of the Bible…to love the Lord their God with all their heart, soul, mind, and strength. Imagine their passionate pursuit of holiness. Imagine their willingness to die for Christ.

This passage, in my opinion, describes the essence of a mature Christian. Bishop McCleod went on to share his vision for men in the body of Christ specifically by writing the following,

Imagine a man or husband or father who loves God with all his heart, mind, soul, and strength. Imagine him working hard, with a long-term vision of where he and his family might be by God's grace. Imagine his priestly pursuit of holiness, refusing to hurt himself and his family through his own unrighteousness, and his willingness to repent quickly when he fails. Imagine how he lovingly, tenderly, but firmly declares God's Word in his home and in the community. If married, imagine how he loves his wife with his whole heart, how he thinks and says she's beautiful, how he covers her, provides for her, protects her, and is literally willing to die for her (*I will add including dying to self*). Imagine how he counts it an honor to lead her, disciple her, and work so that she always feels safe and secure. If a father, imagine a man who teaches and disciples his children. Imagine how he protects them from ungodly influences, instructs them, and casts great vision for who they could be. Imagine how he prays with them and prepares them for adulthood, marriage, and family!

As a man in my midforties, I would be considered by most to be a mature man. Yet as a husband, I am only in my early twenties and likewise as a father. I can recall exhibiting early signs of leadership as I participated in Pop Warner football and on my local Little League baseball team during my preteen years. My earliest memory of being a mentor was in my late teens as an airman (E3) in the United States Navy. I had the opportunity to tutor and mentor the son of one of my coworkers who was struggling with the absence of his father. I mention these years in order to make the point that as I give time and attention to maturing as a man, I need to also give more time and focused attention to maturing as a husband, a father, a leader, and as a mentor.

The Husband

Husbands, love you wives, even as Christ also loved the church, and gave himself for it (Eph. 5:25).

Now as a husband, my wife would probably like the title of this book to read, "God Is Looking for a Mature Man...and so Is My Wife!" I say this jokingly; however, it underscores the need for continuing in the maturation process as a husband. In the context of this message, the *husband* is defined as "the man who enters into a covenant relationship with a woman and becomes responsible for loving, protecting, encouraging, and supporting her; he is to be the band around and covering for their household;

he is the head of household; the strong man."[138] My friend Brian Gullins said it this way, "The husband is the band that is to hold the family together." I had the privilege and honor to enter this covenant relationship with my beautiful wife April, "my queen!" The following is a message April shared during a birthday celebration:

To the man I love,

Dear husband, I love you and I am glad God has blessed you with another year of life. For with each year we spend together we have another chance to grow, another chance to show forth His [God's] purpose in our lives. Thank you for being such a special and cherished part of my life and sharing your God-given years with me. I appreciate you. You are a great father to our children. I know with each year we will continue to grow in love [heart)].

Your partner
Your friend
Your lady
Your love

With all my heart,

Queen

I met April for the first time during the summer of 1989 at a weeklong Christian camp after graduating from high school and before leaving for naval boot camp. As April and her family arrived and were walking up the gravel driveway, the teenage boys' group

---

138   Mark 3:27: "No one can enter a strong man's house and plunder his goods, unless he first binds the strong man. And then he will plunder his house."

was preparing to start an obstacle course. We were introduced by a mutual friend right before I went on to win the obstacle course. I don't recall having any other conversation with her during the remainder of the week; however, about midweek, the guys devised a plan. The plan was to go far off into the woods with the girls and pretend to get lost and then be the heroes as we guide everyone back to camp. Now, what is interesting about this story is that I had not thought about this experience again until after April and I were married for about three years. One night we were talking about the camp experience, and we realized that we had met prior to the winter of 1992 (when we officially started dating). The scripture says, "He who finds a wife finds a good thing,"[139] and I say, "Amen! Amen! And amen again!" April and I married on New Year's Day in 1994, and I am grateful to God for keeping us and keeping our marriage.

While we were engaged to be married, we had established loving names for one another that would remind us of who we were to each other. April was and is my "Queen," and I was and am her "love." When I finally came to realize and understand "who I am" to her, I appreciated that every time she called me Love, she was speaking life into me by reminding me of my identity. Fortunately, I also came to realize that I was falling short of my responsibilities of loving her, protecting her, encouraging her, and supporting her unconditionally and in every aspect of her life. In the process of receiving this revelation, I found that there is a "standard of love"[140] that is required of every mature man, every husband, and every father must live up to it. Like Adam when he blamed Eve, I (in my immature state) did not want to accept the responsibility for not living up to the "standard of love" and obedience to the instructions set by our Heavenly Father.

If the truth be told I have not always adhered to the duties of a mature husband throughout our marriage. For many years I

---

[139] Proverbs 18:22: "He who finds a wife finds a good thing, And obtains favor from the LORD."

[140] 1 Corinthians 13

failed to love April as Christ loves the church. At times, I was not the most mature husband in my actions neither in my speech, but I thank God that Love covers a multitude of faults. In my case, I attempted to love my wife and my family out of my own deficits, fears, and immaturity and I started making a mess. Many times I spoke out of anger and fear not in love and kindness toward my wife. As I draw closer to God, love began to dispel my fears and I was blessed to receive the grace, mercies, and forgiveness of God and my precious Queen.[141] Thank God for His love, kindness, and tender mercies! I thank God for April and my children who never gave up on me through my deficits, fears, and immaturity. I am eternally grateful to them for their love, protection, encouragement, and support. I encourage every husband, in the name of Jesus, to love your wife as Christ loves His church and gave Himself for her.[142] I will close this section with a recent note from my wife found inside one of my Christmas gifts after twenty-two years of marriage:

> For my husband, we made each other promises while standing face to face, and we have kept our wedding vows, because of daily grace. I know that we are not perfect, nor do we need to be, but I am always there for you…as you've been there for me.
>
> Love, Queen

---

[141] 1 John 4:18: "There is no fear in love; but perfect love casts out fear, because fear involves torment. But he who fears has not been made perfect in love."

[142] Ephesians 5:25: "Husbands, love your wives, just as Christ also loved the church and gave Himself for her."

The Father

And you, fathers, do not provoke your children to wrath, but bring them up in the training and admonition of the Lord (Eph. 6:4).

In this text, *fatherhood* is defined as *the covenant relationship between a man and his child (or children); the man is responsible for loving, protecting, encouraging, supporting, training, and affirming his child (or children); the man speaks into the life of his child while guiding him/her toward discovery of their truest spiritual identity, development of their spiritual gifts, and fulfillment of their divine purpose.* I have made the decision to have the words of my children fill this section. I believe it is important to hear the voice of those being fathered. My focus as a father has been and continues to be the fulfillment of the proverb to train up a child in the way they should go.[143] As a father, I have been intentional about loving, protecting, encouraging, supporting, training, and affirming my children as they discover who they are in Christ, develop their gifts and talents, and progress toward

---

[143] Proverbs 22:6: "Train up a child in the way he should go,
And when he is old he will not depart from it."

fulfillment of their life's purpose. The following are shared messages to me from my five children from the oldest to the youngest:

Daddy,

Thank you. Thank you for *every* experience you shared with me. Every one (experience) has played a part in who I am today and how I carry myself. I wouldn't be as resilient to the pressures of life if I hadn't had you as a teacher at home. Thank you for the support: coming to my track meets, honorary events and instilling in me the importance of a hard work ethic. Mistakes are a part of life, but hey, this is your first time being a father, and I'd say you are doing a good job. There are lots of things you would say when I was younger that I understand now as a young adult and are key to lifelong progress, such as "Be a lifelong learner," "Readers are leaders," "Work hard now and it will help you later on," and thinking critically and asking questions. All of these have helped me develop a mind-set that will facilitate my long term goal of being whole and knowing myself. HAPPY FATHER'S DAY. LOVE YOU ALWAYS.

Your firstborn, Janae'
(second to the left)

***

Daddy,

Thank you for all you do for us. From guiding us with our school work and academics, to supporting

94

and cheering for us in our athletics, and teaching us many things vital to every child's life including riding a bike, swimming, and even the simplest of things such as tying our shoes. You have always provided, protected, encouraged, cared for, and loved us...even when it was *tough* love (inside a heart). Thank you for instilling necessary values, and helping to shape the morals and values we will later instill in our own children. You have raised us on a foundation based upon Christ (Jesus) and taught us the importance of knowing *who we are*! Most of all you have given us the greatest thing any parent could give a child, you have invested *time*, and for that I thank you and say I love you and...HAPPY FATHER'S DAY!

Your twin, Janine
(in the middle)

***

Daddddy,

I really appreciate everything you've done for us these past twenty years! I remember the first time you held baby Janae'...what a precious moment (sike = joke) haha :)! [Janette is our middle child and wasn't born yet.] But seriously, thanks for providing, supporting, loving, caring, encouraging and so much more. I can only imagine how hard at times it must be to be a father of five, but if I must say so myself, I think you've done an excellent job. You've instilled in us so many life lessons: "Readers are leaders," "You can lead a horse to water, but you can't make him drink it" :) etc. I'm glad I can say, "I have a father who cares and loves me.' You are an example to us of what a father should be. Thanks for raising us in a Christian-based household (heart). Although I may not say it all the time, I love you, Daddy! HAPPY FATHER'S DAY!

Janette – Babe
(first on left)

***

HAPPY FATHER'S DAY!

Thank you for everything you do for me. Thanks for teaching me how to be a God-fearing man, and guiding and preparing me to lead a family of my own one day. you are a great leader, father, and man. I appreciate the disciplining, the talks, and all the chess games and competition. They push me to be better. I love you for just being you, and also for everything you do…(oooh bars). Thank you for all the love and care you show to us. Even the little things you do make a big difference. Also, thank you for always providing and being there for us. you are a great example of what a father is supposed to be. Thank you.

Love,
Your only son,
John Hatcher IV

***

Daddy,

I'm sooo glad that you are fathering us kids. Thank you for everything you have done for us I appreciate all the times you saved your food and candy for me. You *always* have my back when it comes to food and many more things. Daddy, you have taught us to love God and worship him as we were called to do. You also said we each have a purpose and that we must know our purpose in life! Thanks for providing for our every need and *wants*. Thanks for protecting us and teaching us how a man is supposed to treat a lady. I love you for taking your time and raising us like a real man should. Thank you for not being one of those fathers that leave their kids. I enjoy the rides we go on even (if it is just to pick up someone from work!) I also enjoy the times you take us or just me to the movies. Thanks for loving and caring for us. Thanks for showing us off to your friends because you are so proud of us, but we are really proud of you too. All the times you ever yelled or screamed, I know you didn't mean it you just cared. I love and care about you too. I LOVE U so much! HAPPY FATHER'S DAY.

Luv,
Jasmine Hatcher
The 1 and *only*!
(second to the right)

Prayer: Father, in the name of Jesus, I pray that you would turn the hearts of fathers toward their children[144] and the hearts of the children

---

[144] Malachi 4:6: "And he shall turn the hearts of the fathers to the children, and the heart of the children to their fathers."

toward their fathers; and I pray, Lord Jesus, that every mature father would leave an inheritance to his children's children that is rooted in your love.[145] Thank you, Lord, for hearing and answering our prayer!

The Leader

But he that is greatest among you, let him be as the younger; and he that is chief, as he that doth serve.[146]

In this section I will discuss the role of the man as a leader in the context of his family and in his community. I have defined a *leader* as *one who is responsible for serving, training, guiding, and commissioning others toward fulfillment of a common objective.* John Maxwell, who is a well-known author on the subject of leadership, defined *leadership* as "influence-nothing more, nothing less."[147] Although, I agree that leadership is absolutely about having influence, I would have to further assert that true Christian leadership requires service, training, guidance, and an affirmation that launches those being led.

After moving our family to Virginia and serving at a local church for a few years, my wife and I saw the need to pour into our children spiritually in a very intimate and personal way. We began having Bible study in our home as a family with a yearly plan of going through the Bible. I developed a daily schedule, and we started in the summer of 2010 reading one chapter in the book of Proverbs and two chapters in the book of Psalms each day. My wife, who is a singer/songwriter, wrote on average three to five songs per week throughout that first

---

[145]   Proverbs 13:22: "A good man leaves an inheritance to his children's children."
[146]   Luke 22:26
[147]   http://www.johnmaxwell.com/

summer. During the months of September through December, we read through the New Testament; and at the beginning of January through June we read through the Old Testament. We would read and discuss the text as each family member participated by reading, asking, and answering questions. We began to understand that we were doing what the early priests would do; which is simply read the holy scriptures over and over again.

As we completed the first year of our study, the Holy Spirit revealed that as we continued to engage the word of God through our yearly Bible study we would go from faith to faith and from glory to glory, line upon line, precept upon precept. The revelation was that each time we completed a year of study we would go to another level of learning as a family. So, the first year was the year of (*knowledge and a basic awareness*) of the full context of the sixty-six books. The second year would be a year of deeper understanding (*comprehension*) of God's love letter to man. It was during this second year that we received instruction from the Holy Spirit through a visiting friend that our ministry as a family was found in the scriptural text written by Paul to the Colossians.[148] In essence, our corporate identity calls for us to teach, admonish, and sing as we abide in God's word. It was also during this year that each member of our family assumed the role as one of the pillars in the house of wisdom.[149] I assumed the role of instruction, my wife was understanding, Janae' was assigned to prudence, Janine became knowledge, Janette was assigned as obedience, John IV became discipline, and Jasmine was assigned as discretion. These are the pillars highlighted in the book of Proverbs.

In the third year (application) we had to focus on not just being hearers of God's word but doers.[150] By this time, I had completed my doctorate in education from Regent University. So, by year three of

---

[148]   Colossians 3:16: "Let the word of Christ dwell in you richly in all wisdom; teaching and admonishing one another in psalms and hymns and spiritual songs, singing with grace in your hearts to the Lord."

[149]   Proverbs 9:1: "Wisdom hath builded her house, she hath hewn out her seven pillars."

[150]   James 1:22: "But be ye doers of the word, and not hearers only, deceiving your own selves."

our family Bible study we began investing in studio time in order to produce the songs previously written by my wife and daughters. My wife began sharing her music ministry at concert events and with CDs of her songs. My daughters also wrote and shared their music in local churches and sometimes sang with my wife and other times by themselves. I helped to organize a men's fellowship (Men of Valor) at a local barbershop, conducted a workshop ("The Mature Man") for a local church, and began a mentorship program at a local recreation center. All of which was done with my son at my side as he entered what I call "man training." It was also during this time that I asked the Lord, How He was able to teach and minister to thousands of men, women, and children who were at various levels of learning and meet them at their place of need. The Holy Spirit brought to my attention Bloom's taxonomy, which is a concept that examines levels of learning in the Foundations of Education 101. Bloom's theory that learning begins at the basic knowledge and awareness level and progresses through six levels as the learner engages the information. After the awareness comes an understanding and comprehension and then the learning is applied. The learning is used and then analyzed or broken down into parts. Once learning is broken down into parts it can be merged with other information and synthesized into an enhanced body of knowledge. Lastly, Bloom theorized that at the sixth level of evaluation knowledge is used to make judgments.

The Holy Spirit said as Jesus taught using stories each person could glean from the words of truth based on their level of learning. Little children could interpret the theme of the parable, while others could hone in on a specific part of the message (examples: a specific topic, a sentence, a phrase, and/or just one word) depending on their level of learning. There would also be those who would become the storytellers, writers, and creators based on His truth. Those who operated at this seventh level of learning were doing so in *faith*; then the Holy Spirit said *faith* is knowledge perfected. This means that the revelation came with the example of how most of us learned to ride a bike. As we learned about what a bike was and what it could do (awareness), we began to (understand) that the tire allowed the bike to roll, while the handle bars were used for direction and the pedals helped to create speed (analysis). Our first attempts at riding (application) came with excitement and sometimes fear as we worked to coordinate the different parts of the bike (synthesis). After pushing off different starting points and ending sometimes on the ground we were forced to assess how fast to pedal and how hard to turn (evaluation), while balancing the bike with our excitement as the fear subsided. Finally, after minutes, hours, days, weeks, months, and even years of practice, we got it. We could jump on our bikes without a second thought and go. Some of us began to introduce pop-willies, jumping ramps, and other tricks into our ride. We became masters at manipulating our bikes as we increased our speed, the sharpness of our turns, riding with no hands, and whatever else came to mind. Our experience with learning to ride a bike took us through the six levels of learning and into the seventh level as well. Meaning, years at a time could go by and our faith and experience with riding will allow us to jump right on and go. We have perfected our knowledge of riding a bike to the point that now it is not a second thought to jump on a bike and go when the opportunity presents itself. Our knowledge is perfected with regard to riding a bike. I believe that the Lord desires for every mature man to operate at that seventh level of learning when it comes to His word. When we operate at the faith level[151] and we are presented with situations and circumstances in life we immediately go to our faith in God's word of Truth. As we live in the seventh level of learning, in our spiritual identity, we become the living breathing word of God as mature men. We lead by example as living epistles of Jesus Christ the son of the living God, who became our example.

The Mentor

After this manner therefore pray ye: Our Father which art in heaven, Hallowed be thy name. Thy kingdom come. Thy will be done in earth, as it is in heaven. Give

---

[151]   2 Corinthians 5:7: "For we live by faith, not by sight."

us this day our daily bread. And forgive us our debts, as we forgive our debtors. And lead us not into temptation, but deliver us from evil: For thine is the kingdom, and the power, and the glory, forever. Amen.[152]

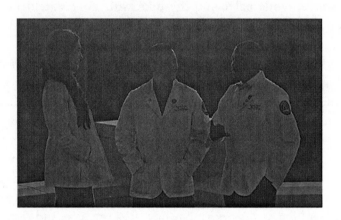

The role of the mentor will now be shared in this section of chapter six. The *mentor* is *that man (or woman) who is in a committed or covenant relationship that is responsible for guiding someone who is less experienced toward discovering their truest spiritual identity and fulfillment of their life's purpose.* Historically, the mentor was the man who was left in the father's stead when the father left for war or went away on a long business trip. The mature man is called to be a father to his children and also a surrogate father to those who are fatherless and need the guidance of someone more experienced. I have had the honor and privilege of being a mentor to many young men in both a formal and informal setting. Below you will find the words of a young man that I had the opportunity to mentor during my tenure as a school administrator in an urban high school in New Jersey. I received the picture above from Dr. Lawrenshey Charles (far right) with two of his residency colleagues along with the following words:

---

[152]   Matthew 6:9–13

Thank you *John Hatcher*. I really appreciate it, but trust me when I say you set the bar high for me. In high school, I looked to you as a great mentor. A well respected man of God in the city. One whose love for his family is evident and a man who is always ready to reach back to those in need despite their appearance and/or attitude. I remember conversations we shared about doing good, living healthy, and soaring like eagles. These conversations have stayed with me and I aspire to turn them into actions and habits every day. So once again Dr. John Hatcher, from the bottom of my heart...THANK YOU!"

Dr. Lawrenshey Charles (Former Student)

Dr. Lawrenshey Charles was a student at Irvington High School in Irvington New Jersey where I was afforded my first opportunity as a public school administrator. The cities of Irvington, Orange, and surrounding Newark were all plagued with gang violence at the time. I recall losing a number of students involved in homicides as a result of this violence and subsequently attending funeral services for some of these young people. I remember praying to God at one service and asking the Lord why am I here and feeling like I was a part of the problem if I couldn't be a part of the solution. That night the Holy Spirit gave me the name of a group for young people that would focus on mentoring in the areas of personal development and character education.

As a result, the Sons of Promise and Daughters of Destiny (SOP and DOD)[153] group was born at Irvington High School and sponsored by Officer Akilah Horton, Ms. Rita Owens, and myself. Lawrenshey and about fifteen other students were already student leaders in a larger student group; yet they were eager for more. So, we began to mentor this smaller more intimate group using the

---

[153]   Galatians 4:21–30

wellness concept for personal development and character traits, such as, respect, responsibility, and resilience. I remember Dr. Charles emerging from this SOP and DOD group as a strong, positive, and determined young man. Although Lawrenshey had more support from his family than most, I had the distinct privilege of serving as a mentor to him. There are many young people like Lawrenshey who could benefit from the wisdom, insight, and guidance of an experienced and available mentor. Many of these young people are without any system of support. As Christian men, we have an example in Jesus Christ of how to be intentional mentors who also disciple in the faith.

Jesus took three years to mentor and disciple His followers as he advised them on how to approach God the Father in prayer. He communicated the Lord's Prayer;[154] which instructs us as Christian believers on how to approach God the Father through prayer and worship in the spirit. This prayer gives specific steps for us to take as we move through the tabernacle in pursuit of the Holy One. As stated previously, the role of the mentor historically has been that of the man who stands in the gap for fathers in their absence. The mentor's responsibility is to train, advise, encourage, and support his mentee wherever he maybe in his life. It is absolutely crucial for the mentor to establish a mutually respectful and trusting relationship with his mentee. The difference between the role of the mentor and that of the father can be easily understood by referring back to the different types of relationships in chapter 2. The mentor/mentee relationship is usually understood to be a casual or a committed relationship with the potential of developing into a covenant relationship, as I believe I have established with Dr. Charles as a Son of Promise. Mentoring, in my opinion, is like discipling in that the responsibilities to train, advise, encourage, and support are all the same. *Discipling* is

---

[154]   Matthew 6:9–13, Matthew 6:9–13: "In this manner, therefore, pray: Our Father in heaven, Hallowed be Your name. Your kingdom come. Your will be done. On earth as it is in heaven. Give us this day our daily bread. And forgive us our debts, As we forgive our debtors. And do not lead us into temptation, But deliver us from the evil one. For Yours is the kingdom and the power and the glory forever. Amen."

a *developmental process of strictly adhering to the instructions of Jesus Christ; which requires one to train, advise, encourage, support, and commission.* How mentoring and discipling differ is that the added responsibility of the master teacher doing the discipling is to also commission the disciple to go forth and share the gospel.

The roles of the husband, the father, the leader, and the mentor are all critical relationships that many mature men will engage during their lifetime. Men are charged by our creator God to be the repairers of the breach and the restorers of paths to dwell in.[155] It is important for men to know, understand, and fulfill the duties assigned with these crucial roles in our families and communities. The next section of the chapter presents an assignment involving four questions that I posed to some of the most mature men I know and includes their responses.

Here's the Assignment:

As a mature man in Christ, consider the following questions in the context of scripture and your personal experience. There is no expectation of word count; however, your responses should be as clear and concise as possible. The following four (4) questions are posed for you to respond to using scripture and your personal experience.

1. **What does it mean to be a loving husband?**
2. **What does it mean to be a godly father?**
3. **What does it mean to be a service-oriented leader?**
4. **What does it mean to be a spiritual mentor?**

The following responses are quoted from five men who I esteem highly and believe to be mature men of God. Dr. Carlos Campo (Dr. C. C.), Pastor Carlthaniel Crum (Pastor C. C.), Bro. Nelson Diaz (Bro. N. D.), Bishop Carlton McCleod (Bishop C. M.), and Bro. Joseph McDaniel (Bro. J. D.) are all, in my opinion, mature men

---

[155]   Isaiah 58:12

of God who are leaders in their families and communities. These men represent over 250 years of life experience, almost 120 years of marriage, they are fathers to sixteen children (to date), and their love for Jesus Christ becomes immediately evident in an encounter with anyone one of them. Their responses to the four questions are listed by question and in the order they are mentioned above:

What does it mean to be a loving husband?[156]

To be a loving husband means to love your wife sacrificially, "as Christ loved the Church and gave Himself for it." It means to put her needs before your own, and to be intentional about ensuring that she reaches her fullest potential in Christ. A loving husband challenges his wife—as you would anyone you loved—to be better, closer to Jesus, always seeking Him at the center of all you do. A loving husband understands that love is a verb, and demands action. It is an act of the will, not a feeling. It is a daily decision that says, "I *will* love you today, just as I promised before God and my peers, and every other day that the Lord gives me breath to fulfill the privilege of being your husband."

A loving husband reserves the "first fruits" of his words, deeds, time, talent and treasure for her—the one for whom you have "forsaken all others" (Dr. C. C.).

A loving husband, sacrifices for his spouse he is willing to compromise, listen and lay down his life for his spouse, and also make his spouse feel protected and secure. A Husband should love his wife as much as *Christ* loved the church and gave *His* life for it…And there is more implied in the words than mere protection and support, for as *Christ* gave *Himself* for the church to save it, so husbands should, by all means in their power, labor to promote the salvation of their wives, and their constant edification in righteousness (Pastor C. C.).

To love *all* of me which includes my wife as we are one and to pursue her wellness which is paramount for God's purpose to be

---

156   Ephesians 5:25: "Husbands, love your wives, just as Christ also loved the church and gave Himself for her."

fulfilled in us individually and as a union. To place the same value on my wife as God does for His daughter. To support her as my equal understanding that God has placed her in my life to be a bridle and fuel which are both necessary for confirmation as well as for when my spiritual senses have been dulled. To remember that our communication is usually a reflection of my communication with God. Evelyn has helped me avoid several train wrecks which my foresight failed to see coming due to my excitement, ambitions, and even my eagerness to do the work of the Lord (Bro. N. D).

To be a loving husband is to love one's wife as Christ loves the church. God, who is love, gets to define love. So it is critical that a godly and loving husband take his "love" cues from Christ Himself. A loving husband must "give himself up" for his wife. He must protect her holiness. He must wash her daily with the Word of God. He must desire to see her and count her as beautiful. He must consider how he might treat his own self, and love her likewise. In essence, he must be priest and prophet, provider and protector. And he must do these things with kindness, care, fidelity, and honor! (Bishop C. M.).

It means that I have a responsibility to duplicate the role and passion of Jesus Christ, which is to love my wife life as Christ loves the church—as he died and gave himself for her. To give my life for her—my time, gifts, talents and abilities for the benefit of sustaining, caring and providing for her. To nurture her and to serve her to the point where she fulfills her destiny, walks in her uniqueness and is free from anything that is ungodly—according to the washing of the water of the Word of God. As such, to protect and cover her—both spiritually and physically. To pray with her and for her. To declare God's Word over her. To speak life into her. To affirm her and everything about her—including affirming her children. The woman is the weaker vessel. Because of this, Peter says, I am to honor her. To understand her. To treat her as my equal, so that my prayers won't be hindered. To perfect her, to develop her, to mature her, to feed her, care for her in order to present her to myself without spot or wrinkle. To present her as a perfected jewel—reflecting of the heart of her husband and the glory of God. To passionately promote her expecting and wishing everything for her that I would wish for myself. To put her before myself. This also means to place her desires ahead of my own—as long as this does not conflict with obedience to the Holy Spirit. To never embarrass her or disrespect her. To favor her, more than I favor anyone else. To highly value and consider her thoughts, convictions and suggestions. To be one with her (Bro. J. D.).

What does it mean to be a godly father?[157]

To be a godly father is to model Christ in all you do, to "have this attitude that was in Christ Jesus," and "empty yourself" in obedience to God's call in your life. A godly father is relentless in helping his daughter or son to fulfill the destiny for which they were created. A godly father helps his children understand they have an enemy of their souls, and that they must resist him and the seductive power of conformity to this world. A godly father leads by example in cherishing daily time with Jesus, valuing Scripture as God's revealed Word, and walking in humility, truth and grace (Dr. C. C.).

A Godly father is one who teaches his children the ways of *God* as he walks in the ways of *God* before them. Proverbs 22:6 Teach your children right from wrong, and when they are all grown they will still do right. When he comes to the opening of the way of life, being able to walk alone, and to choose, stop at this entrance, and begin a series of instructions, how he is to conduct himself in every step he takes (Pastor C. C.).

To provide your children a secure structure for eternal success mirrored after God's fathering in Genesis where the rewards and repercussions were defined well before the children had any decisions to make. To exercise compassion, forgiveness, grace, & mercy as often as the opportunities arise. To disciple your children to do the same. I created too many relationship barriers with my children when my fathering was reactive until I began to follow

---

[157] Ephesian 4:6: "And you, fathers, do not provoke your children to wrath, but bring them up in the training and admonition of the Lord."

Father God's proactive ways. I must admit that I am still trying to navigate the choppy waters created by my reactive backseat-driver parenting. (Bro. N. D.).

A godly father, again, desires to follow Scripture in his fatherhood. A godly father first desire is to see his children walking with Christ. He therefore studies great passages like Deuteronomy 6, Psalms 78, Ephesians 6, and the book of Proverbs to learn what he must do. A godly father loves, instructs, encourages, disciples, protects, models, disciplines, and prays for and with his children. He enjoys them and has times of rejoicing with them. He sees in them generations that must also be discipled and builds his home and discipleship accordingly. He understands that he has been given the responsibility by God to shepherd and oversee living souls made in the image of God. His children are his joy, and it shows! (Bishop C. M.).

It means that I have a responsibility to duplicate the role and passion of Jesus Christ, which is to be fruitful and multiply. To be fruitful is to reproduce and to present for nourishment all that is placed within you. The role of the father is to pass on his own DNA— his seed, which came from the ultimate DNA—God Almighty. God said, let us make man in our image and likeness. Fathers are to protect the DNA of God, to ensure that we pass on the fullness of God's potent seed to our children – spiritual and natural children. To study the image and likeness of God. In doing so, we are to protect our children from an erred image and likeness. To accomplish this, we have to study, know and obey the Holy Scriptures. Fathers are to love our children and not to provoke them to anger by treating them negatively or harshly. We are to respect them and to love them and God's seeds in the earth. Encourage my children to pursue the salvation of Jesus Christ. Matt. 18:3: "But if you cause one of these little ones who trusts me to fall into sin, it would be better for you to have a large millstone tied around your neck and be drowned in the depths of the sea." Matthew 18:6 To hold godly reverence for them, as they are the children of the Lord. Finally, Paul says that fathers are to discipline them and to instruct them, with the instructions from the Lord (Bro. J. M.).

What does it mean to be a service-oriented leader?

A service-oriented leader is outwardly focused in all he or she does. They pledge to follow Christ's ten-word dictum of discipleship: "Deny yourself, take up your cross daily, and follow me." Self-denial—not from a legalistic mind-set but one of love—is the starting point for every servant leader. In a world that calls us to place the self above all else, Christ knows that we must "daily" die to self, or "take up our cross," in order to truly walk with Him. Following Christ is easy if we deny ourselves and take up our cross daily. It is impossible if we do not (Dr. C. C.).

A service-oriented leader is one who serves the needs of those whom he leads as well as being of service to those he comes in contact with within his community. John 13:5: *He* put some water into a large bowl, then *He* began washing his disciples' feet and drying them with the towel *He* was wearing. This act is symbolic of spiritual cleansing as well as a model of the attitude believers are to adopt towards one another especially leaders (Pastor C. C.).

To be sacrificial in word and deed. To invest your time, talents, and treasures in the service of man, as a working example to others for the glory of God. To lead and align others, in every divinely appointed opportunity, to their place of service in God's kingdom here on earth. An increase in kingdom productivity is usually found when someone teaches others the importance of their service as opposed to doing things totally on their own (Bro. N. D.)

A service-oriented leader models himself after Jesus. He is aware first of all of his sinfulness and depravity, and from that place of humility has the right temperament and countenance to serve others in a Christ-exhorting way. He never "lords over;" he never manipulates; he isn't out for personal gain or personal kingdom building. On the contrary, he desires to see others released into fruitfulness and the kingdom of Christ strengthened as a result. He is quick to assume responsibility for bad decisions; quick to forgive; and quick to be self-effacing. He is also quick to share success and deflect praise. He sees his leadership as an "offering" to the Lord and he isn't' confused about the nature of success: faithfulness! (Bishop C. M.).

It means that I have a responsibility to duplicate the role and passion of Jesus Christ in laying down my life for my friend. John 15:13. Jesus is the ultimate servant leader, having come down from Glory to put himself in our shoes. Hebrew 4:15 Therefore, we are to put ourselves in the position of others. In doing so, we position ourselves to understand them. Mark 12:31 Love your neighbor as yourself. "Give to anyone who asks; and when things are taken away from you, don't try to get them back. Do to others as you would like them to do to you." Luke 6:30 Jesus said, "This is my command: Love each other." John 15:13 NLT. To lead is to love, to love is to sacrifice—your life for others. To lead is to serve, to give everything that you have to aid, better, develop, influence, direct and encourage others (Bro. J. M.).

What does it mean to be a spiritual mentor?

To be a spiritual mentor begins with intentionality regarding the transmission of eternal spiritual values to another. A spiritual mentor must be transparent, open to the Spirit is leading, and communicate clearly to the mentee. A spiritual mentor must realize that he or she is not a receptacle, but a conduit for God's blessing and truth. A mentor seeks the Lord for direction, wisdom and truth, and then pours this out to others. They allow the "rivers of living water" to flow through them to others (Dr. C. C.).

A spiritual mentor is one who helps mentor not only his children, but also those who he comes in contact with, that just need someone to share the things of the spirit with them, for lack of having someone in their life to lead and guide them in the things of *God.* 1 Corinthians 2:13 Every word we speak was taught to us by *God's* spirit, not by human wisdom. And this same spirit helps us teach spiritual things to spiritual people. We must speak the things of *God* in the words of *God*, everything plain and intelligible; every word well placed and clear. He who has a spiritual mind will easily comprehend this teaching (Pastor C. C.).

To be trustworthy with the spiritual nurturing of others based on a proven track record of faithfulness and maturity in Christ that can be confirmed at a glance by witnessing your home/family life (Bro. N. D.).

A good mentor, first of all, loves the one he is mentoring. He truly wants to see them grow in Christ and be passionate about the things of God. He recognizes that the nature of mentoring is similar to parenting. While some "mentors" seem to want to *be* served, a good spiritual mentor realizes that he is there *to* serve. He gives freely of his time. He prays for the mentee. He sets an example and says "follow me." He models, helps the mentee execute, and then observes as the mentee "goes it alone," offering counsel and guidance. He also is unwilling to take credit for any successes of his student but may graciously say "thank you" if it is offered. He feels as if he succeeds if his student does. He even knows when to release them to others when the time is right, and without jealously. These kinds of mentors are hard to find! (Bishop C. M.).

It means that I have a responsibility to duplicate the role and passion of Jesus Christ, in imitating His own Father. Jesus said, "Whatever the Father does, the Son also does. For the Father loves the Son and shows him everything he is doing." John 5:19, 20 Follow me, as I follow Christ. The New Living Translation says, "And, you should imitate me, just as I imitate Christ." 1 Cor. 11:1 Paul, a great mentor said, "For even if you have ten thousand others who teach you about Christ, you have only one spiritual father. For, I became your father in Christ Jesus when I preached the Good News to you. So, I urge you to imitate me." 1 Cor. 4:15. A spiritual mentor is to encourage those they serve to imitate them, as they follow and imitate Christ themselves first. Spiritual mentors are to be examples of Christ's image, likeness, and character. As a spiritual mentor it means to "Imitate God, therefore, in everything you do, because you are his dear children. Live a life filled with love, following the example of Christ. He loved us and offered himself as a sacrifice for us, a pleasing aroma to God. To be a spiritual mentor means to imitate God, and encourage your spiritual children to imitate you (Bro. J. M.).

I am thankful to these mature men of God for offering their earnest thoughts on the previously posed questions. Individually and collectively they have provided some great insight that is rooted in God's holy word! How men fulfill their duties associated with the roles they play in the lives of their family members, as well as, their communities will always have a great impact on both. I would caution and encourage every man to be accountable to these roles from a foundation rooted in *love* and not out of fear. If the duties associated with these roles are not engaged through *love*, then the man will attempt to satisfy his responsibilities from a place of fear. This will lead to one bad decision after another, which will not result in the love, protection, encouragement, and support needed in each relationship. The impact of these relationships can be positive or negative depending on the man's success or failure to meet the duties assigned to each.

Prayer: Father, I pray in the name of your son Jesus Christ that you would touch the hearts of your man-servants and that they would be encouraged to love their wives as you love your church. I pray that fathers would train their children and bring them up in the fear and admonition of You. Help us, Lord, to serve our families and community in a manner that honors you and encourage our hearts to stand in the gap for those coming after us. Help us to guide them toward their purpose in You. Thank you Lord Jesus for helping us to be better men in Jesus's name. Amen!

CHAPTER 7

Let Every Man Examine Himself

Brethren, be not children in understanding: howbeit in malice be ye children, but in understanding be men (1 Cor. 14:20).

That we [henceforth] be no more children, tossed to and fro, and carried about with every wind of doctrine, by the sleight of men, [and] cunning craftiness, whereby they lie in wait to deceive (Eph. 4:14–15).

Till we all come in the unity of the faith, and of the knowledge of the Son of God, unto a perfect man, unto the measure of the stature of the fullness of Christ (Eph. 4:13).

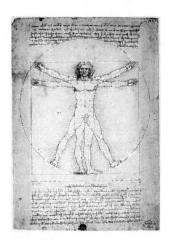

The Measure of a Man

This final chapter is an opportunity for self-examination of your life as it relates to your development toward maturity as a man. Let every man examine himself and determine where he is regarding key aspects of life related to the process of maturity associated with manhood.[158] This chapter will help you to assess where you are with regard to:

- your relationship with God
- your clarity about your identity and purpose in God
- yourself in each of the six aspects of health
- your duties as a man
- the four key roles in a man's life

This chapter highlights the major points made throughout each of the previous five chapters to allow you (the reader) to rate yourself according to the critical patterns pertaining to man's maturity. When rating yourself the author recommends that you synthesize the scriptural context of each aspect of life, your personal knowledge and experience, and some expert references on each topic. The following section provides an opportunity for you to respond to the question, "Where are you?"

Man's Relationship with God:[159]

A mature man is one who *loves unconditionally*[160] with his whole heart, his mind, his body, and with all his soul (Matt. 22:37–39):

✓ He loves his God
✓ He loves his family
✓ He loves his community (neighbor)

---

[158] 1 Corinthians 11:28: "But let a man examine himself…"
[159] Genesis 3:9
[160] Matthew 22:37–39

In the discussion of where man is in his relationship with God, we used the order of the tabernacle described in the book of Genesis chapter 26 and the book of Exodus chapter 25 to assess the relationship types man can have with God. There are four specific types of relationships discussed in chapter 2 and all of them are in reference to the order of the tabernacle. Man's position in reference to the tabernacle indicates where he is in his relationship with God and with the understanding that God is in the Holy of holies. The first type of relationship man has with God is positioned outside of the tabernacle and is that of the un-repented sinner.[161] The un-repented sinner is the only relationship type discussed that is totally out of fellowship with God, meaning man's relationship with God is nonexistent. The un-repented sinner is living contrary to the will of God and either knowingly or unknowingly has not decided to turn toward God and accept Jesus Christ as his Lord and Savior.

The next three relationship types discussed in this section are inside the tabernacle and they represent man in fellowship with God. In these three relationships man is considered to be inside the ark of safety and members of the body of Christ (Eph. 4:12). In order for man to be in fellowship with God one must fulfill the scriptures found in John 1:12 and Romans 10:9-10. When man believes in God, receives God into his heart, and confesses that Jesus Christ is Lord he enters into fellowship with God as a son (Rom. 8:15). Hence, the second relationship type is the casual son; which is represented in the tabernacle by the outer court. This relationship is the result of man hearing the words of faith (Rom. 10:17), repenting of his sins at the altar of God, and being washed at the laver. Although man is now in fellowship with God, God's desire is still for man to draw closer to Him.

The third relationship type is the committed son, and it is represented in the tabernacle by the inner court also known as the Holy Place. The committed son has passed through the outer court

---

[161]   Psalm 51:5

and is working out his own soul salvation with fear and trembling (Phil. 2:12). The spiritual senses that are at work in the Holy Place are one's sense of taste, one's ability to see, and the sense of smell (Ps. 34:8 and Eph. 5:2). The sense of taste is at work when man partakes of the fruit of the spirit (Gal. 5:22 and 23) in his daily walk. The demonstration of these fruits in a man's life are the evidence that he has tasted the bread of life (John 6:35) from the table of shewbread. The ability to see is accomplished when one's direction in life is guided by the word of God (Ps. 119:105). The sense of seeing refers to the revelation, illumination, and guidance that comes through engaging the word of God (Matt. 6:22 and James 1:25). Jesus Christ becomes man's guide as he continues to draw man closer to God from the light of the candlestick. The sense of smell is in operation as man offers up sincere prayers and acceptable offerings; which are emblematical of one experiencing God through communion at the Altar of Incense also known as the Golden Altar (Ps. 141:2, Eph. 5:2, and Revelations 8:4). These prayers and offerings become a sweet aroma in God's nostrils as they are lifted up towards the heavens. The committed son is closer to God than the casual son, yet there is still room to draw closer to the Holy One.

The fourth relationship type is the covenant son and it is represented in the tabernacle by the Holy of holies. The covenant son has traveled from the outer court, through the inner court, and he has gone beyond the veil into the most Holy place where God is. The covenant son is in the position where he can touch God because, he worships the Lord in spirit and in truth (John 4:24). The covenant son develops the type of relationship with God the Father that God Himself desires of all his children (Rom. 8:16, John 4:23–24, and James 4:8–10). God desires that all his children would draw close to him and touch him, just as the woman who pressed to touch the hem of Jesus's garment (Matt. 9:21). The covenant son is an heir and joint heir to the promises of God with our Lord Jesus Christ. Check the numbered line that best represents your assessment of your current relationship with God the Father given the four relationship types discussed.

Where are you in your relationship with God the Father?

A rating of 1 represents the strongest possible response for a mature man and a rating of 4 represents the weakest possible rating.

1. My relationship with the Lord is that of a

___ 1) covenant son who worships in spirit and in truth and in reverence and in awe; who is in touch with the Holy Spirit frequently (*John 4:23–24*).

___ 2) committed son who has tasted and seen the goodness of the Lord and has a dedicated disciplined prayer life (*Phil. 2:12*).

___ 3) Casual son who has heard the word of faith and has received the salvation of the Lord (*Rom. 10:17*).

___ 4) unrepented sinner who is out of fellowship with the Lord (*Ps. 51:5*).

Identity and Purpose (Jer. 1:5, Jer. 29:11, and Matt. 28:19 and 20)

A mature man is one who *knows who he is*, he *understands his purpose in life*, and *uses his time, talent/s, and treasure toward fulfillment of that same purpose.*

In the beginning and before the foundations of the world God spoke into the spirit of man and told him who he was. In essences God uploaded our identity in the spirit realm and gave each of us gifts and talents in order to fulfill the purpose for which he called us. There are two very important questions that every person needs to answer as they engage the process of maturity. These questions are fundamental and universal regardless of one's cultural background or the circumstances into which one is born. These questions have everything to do with whether one lives a successful life or a life full of failures. The first question that must be answered with clarity is, "Who am I?" The scripture found in Hosea 4:6 says, *My people perish because of lack of knowledge.* This is God speaking to man and letting him know that if he doesn't discover the root of knowledge he will be destroyed.

So what is the root of knowledge? God is the root of all knowledge. God is omniscient, meaning He is omni (or all) science (the study of knowledge) or all-knowing. The message from this scripture is that man will perish if he does not know God. If man does not know God, then man cannot and will not know himself. Any man that does not know himself will not be able to answer the second question, which is, "What is my purpose?" In order to live a successful life man must fulfill his purpose in life. Before man can fulfill his purpose in life he must know who he is. Prior to discovering the knowledge of one's self, one must first know who God is. The scripture found in Matthew 28:18–20...Every man must humble himself and seek the face of God in order to discover his own spiritual identity and his divine purpose. Check the numbered line that best represents your assessment of your spiritual identity and life purpose given the four choices listed.

Where are you in regard to knowing your spiritual identity and fulfilling your life's purpose?

2. When it comes to my spiritual identity (Jer. 1:5),

__ 1) I have explored and committed to my identity; I am sure of who I am and I have a scriptural reference that speaks to my identity in the body of Christ.

__ 2) I have explored and committed to my identity. I am confident in who I am but I have not discovered a specific scripture that speaks to my identity.

__ 3) I have explored or committed (not both) to my identity. I am not totally confident about who I am and/or I feel unsure by what others say about me and/or what I believe about myself.

__ 4) I have neither explored nor committed to my identity. I am confused about who I am and/or I have not thought much about the topic.

3. As far as my purpose in life goes (Matthew 28:18-20),

__ 1) I am absolutely clear about my life's purpose and I am walking completely in my calling.

__ 2) I am sure about my life's purpose and I have started working to fulfill my call.

__ 3) I think I know what my life's purpose is, but I have not started working towards fulfilling it.

__ 4) I have no idea of what my life's purpose is and/or I haven't done much to discover my call.

A mature man is one who lives a well-balanced life:

- He is physically educated, health literate, and understands how to maximize and maintain the strength of his body.
- He has studied and mastered his work.
- He understands his roles and responsibilities in a variety of healthy and appropriate relationships; while having the ability to love, protect, encourage, and support those with whom he has a relationship.
- He knows and understands how to manage, subdue, and express his passions according to love and righteousness.
- He knows and understands his value and worth; he is a good steward over all that is given to his charge.
- He is a covenant Son of God who has established a true intimacy with his heavenly father.

Physical Health - Do you not know that your bodies are temples of the Holy Spirit, who is in you, whom you have received from God? You are not your own; [20] you were bought at a price. Therefore honor God with your bodies (*I Cor. 6:19-20*).

Physical health is the first aspect of health to be assessed with regard to the question "Where are you?" Physical health is the quality of life related to the condition of one's body. The word of God informs us that our bodies are the temple of the Holy Spirit; which simply means that we must prepare ourselves for the spirit of God to dwell in us (1 Cor. 6:19–20). Physical maturity is a physiological process that naturally occurs over time as the systems of the body complete their developmental processes. Every cell in the body has a divine order according to its creative design. The scripture lets us know that the whole body is fitly joined; which is emblematical of the body of Christ (Eph. 4:16). Like cells in our own body have a specific place and a specific function, so it is, that we have a specific place and function in the body of Christ. Romans 12:1 communicates that we must present our bodies as living sacrifices holy and acceptable unto God and this is our reasonable service. There are some important things we must pay attention to when preparing ourselves for the master's use. Here we examine four key components that have the potential to greatly impact one's physical health status. The four components are nutritional status, fitness level, rest, and hygiene.

Assessing one's *nutritional status* requires that an individual should consider their ideal body weight, the recommended daily allowance, and dietary history (Maqbool, Olsen, and Stallings, 2008). Nutritional status is extremely important when assessing overall physical health (1 Cor. 10:31). Another very important component of physical health is an individual's *fitness level*. Assessing fitness level provides the individual with the necessary information about the body's efficiency and performance (www.adultfitness.org). The daily performance and work requires one to rest and rejuvenate the body (Phil. 2:12). *Rest* is essential to the continuous healing process of the body (Exodus 23:12). The Mayo Clinic suggests seven to eight hours of rest for adults (www. sleepfoundation.org). The final component used here to assess overall physical heath is *hygiene* (1 Thess. 5:23). *Merriam-Webster* online defines *hygiene* as "the condition or practice (as of cleanliness) conducive to health" (www.meriam-webster.com). The purpose of hygiene primarily is to rid the body of germs and other disease causing agents. The four components presented here are used to assess the mature man's physical health status with given consideration of his physical age.

Where are you in reference to the strength and maintenance of your body?

Use the previous descriptions to assess each individual component of your physical health. Check the numbered line that best represents your assessment of your physical health given the four variables discussed.

4. When it comes to my *physical health* (1 Cor. 6:19–20, Eph. 4:16, Rom. 12:1, and Ps. 91),

___ 1) I am making healthy food choices, my fitness level is high, I am getting six to eight hours of rest each day, and I pay close attention to my daily hygiene and grooming.

___ 2) I am out of balance with regard to at least one of these four variables.

___ 3) I am out of balance with regard to at least two of these four variables.

___ 4) I am out of balance with regard to at least three of these four variables.

The following scriptural references are additional text related to the body: (Eph. 2:21, 1 Cor. 12:27, Mark 6:31–32, John 9:4, Gen. 3:19, 1 Cor. 10:31, Mat. 26:26, Gal. 5:22–23, and Isa. 58:6).

Mental Health - Do not conform to the pattern of this world, but be transformed by the renewing of your mind. Then you will be able to test and approve what God's will is—his good, pleasing and perfect will (*Romans 12:2*).

Mental health is the second aspect of health to be assessed with regard to the "Where are you?" question. Mental health refers to the quality and state of our minds. When we began to understand the words and the instruction of Christ, then we are developing towards mental maturity. Mental maturity is demonstrated through the transformation of our carnal minds into alignment with the spiritual mind of Christ. The key components of mental health assessed here are learning, meditation, critical thinking, and strategic planning.

Evaluating one's level of learning is crucial to assessing the maturity of one's mind. *Learning* is a process of engaging a body of knowledge that leads to mastery of that same body of knowledge (2 Tim. 2:15). There are six levels of learning that one experiences as he progresses toward maturity within a discipline area (www.successcenter.truman.edu). *Meditation* can be defined as a deliberate process of reflecting and focusing on a single topic. Meditation facilitates deeper levels of learning and promotes mastery of the subject matter; which usually leads to successful use of the learned material (Josh. 1:8).

Critical thinking is a key component of mental health that demonstrates the mental maturity one must possess in order to engage this intellectual process (Eccl. 12:13). The Critical Thinking Foundation defines critical thinking as "the intellectually disciplined process of actively and skillfully conceptualizing, applying, analyzing, synthesizing, and/or evaluating information gathered from, or generated by, observation, experience, reflection, reasoning, or communication, as a guide to belief and action" (www.criticalthinking.org). The mature man is a critical thinker, as well as, a strategic planner. *Strategic planning* is a part of mental health that involves developing steps to accomplish a goal. (Hab. 2:2 and Luke 14:28). The purpose of strategic planning is to focus efforts and maximize resources in order to fulfill a vision. Like playing the game of chess, the mature man must participate in strategic planning in order to fulfill his purpose in life.

Where are you in regard to the development and transformation of your mind?

Use the previous descriptions and use the scales below to assess each individual component of your mental health. Check the numbered line that best represents your assessment of your mental health given the four mental processes discussed.

5. When it comes to my *mental health* (2 Tim. 2:15 and Rom. 12:2),

__ 1) I have studied to show myself approved unto God, my mind has been transformed to the mind of Christ, and I have a sound mind. I am a critical and strategic thinker.
__ 2) I am out of balance with regard to at least one of these four variables.
__ 3) I am out of balance with regard to at least two of these four variables.
__ 4) I am out of balance with regard to at least three of these four variables.

II Peter 1:13; studying (2 Tim. 2:15), meditating (Josh. 1:8 and Psalm 5), critical thinking (Eccl. 12:13), and strategic planning (Luke 14:28).

Social health - "Teacher, which is the greatest commandment in the Law? Jesus replied: "'Love the Lord your God with all your heart and with all your soul and with all your mind.' This is the first and greatest commandment. And the second is like it: 'Love your neighbor as yourself.' All the Law and the Prophets hang on these two commandments"(*Mat. 22:36-40).*

The third aspect of health to be assessed with regard to the "Where are you?" question is social health; which focuses on relationships. The key components of social health that will be assessed here are communication, cooperation, conflict resolution, and manners. *Communication* is an important part of any relationship and is necessary for all relationships to progress toward intimacy (1 Thess. 5:17). Engaging in effective communication requires the mature man to express his thoughts, feelings, and ideas, as well as listening to and interpreting the thoughts, feelings, and ideas of others. The three parts of communication include a sender, a message, and a receiver (www.dalecarnegie.com). One must assess their ability to effectively communicate in a variety of relationship types. *Cooperation* can be defined simply as mutual effort with regard to a common objective (www.thesaurus.com). The saying, "No man is an island unto himself" suggests that all men, at some point, need to connect with others in order to accomplish some objective (Matt. 18:20). A mature man understands that cooperation is an important component of social health. Likewise, conflict resolution is an important component of social heath necessary for maintaining healthy relationships. *Conflict resolution* is a process of resolving conflicts that ensures the relationship remains the priority as pressures build (www.mindtools.com). As personal relationships develop, conflicts will surface which provide opportunities to maintain and strengthen these relationships (Matt. 18:15-17). *Manners* are the final component of social health to be assessed in this section. In our daily interactions with other people there are some minimal expectations for a mature individual (Matt. 7:12). The mature man has a basic respect for all people in a diverse and ever-changing society (www.emilypost.com).

Where are you in the development and maintenance of your healthy and appropriate relationships?

Use the previous descriptions and the scales below to assess each individual component of your social health. Check the numbered line that best represents your assessment of your social health given the four components discussed.

6. When it comes to my *social health* (*Mat. 22:36–40*).

___ 1) I love the Lord with all my heart, mind, body, and soul; I love my neighbor as myself; I am an effective communicator; I work well with others and I am effective at resolving conflicts. I interact with other in a manner that is socially acceptable.

___ 2) I am out of balance with regard to at least one of these four variables.

___ 3) I am out of balance with regard to at least two of these four variables.

___ 4) I am out of balance with regard to at least three of these four variables.

Social health (relationships), communication (1 Thess. 5:17), cooperation (1 Thess. 5:11), conflict resolution (Matt. 18:15–17), and mannerisms (Matt. 7:12).

Emotional Health - Take delight in the Lord, and he will give you the desires of your heart *(Psalms 37:4)*.

The fourth aspect of health to be assessed with regard to the "Where are you?" question is emotional health; which relates to one's feelings. The key components of emotional health that will be assessed here are love, fear, excitement, and anger. *Love* is the first and most important component of emotional health. Love is also the most important component of overall personal wellness and expands throughout all aspects of health (Matt. 22:37–39 and 1 Cor. 13:1–13). Meaning, love can be expressed physically, mentally, socially, emotionally, economically, and spiritually. The mature man understands how to appropriately express his love in a variety of relationships to include; his relationship with God, his family, and his neighbor/s. *Fear* is the next component assessed in regards to emotional health and it is contrary to love (1 John 4:18). Fear is an emotion that causes one to feel threatened or in danger (www.humanillness.com). The mature man is not timid but, is strong, loving, and self-disciplined (2 Tim. 1:7). The only fear that supports one in pursuit of purpose is the fear of God (Ps. 115:11). *Excitement* is another component of emotional health that is helpful when fulfilling purpose. When a man has matured to the point of knowing his spiritual identity and fulfilling his purpose in life there is an excitement that is unmatched when it comes to his work (Ps.

69:9). The mature man that has discovered his calling is motivated to do the work required to fulfill his call even if he didn't get paid for it. The mature man might live according to a motto such as "Lord give me life until my work is done and give me work until my life shall end." The final component of emotional health is anger. *Anger* is a strong feeling of displeasure or hostility (www.thefreedictionary. com). *Anger* can be a very dangerous emotion because it can cause one to bypass the use of good judgment. The mature man manages his anger in a way that addresses the source of displeasure without sinning.

Where are you in regard to your expression and management of your emotions?

Use the previous descriptions to assess each individual component of emotional health and rate your overall emotional stability. Check the numbered line that best represents your assessment of your emotional health given the four emotions discussed.

7. When it comes to my emotional health,

___ 1) I have mastered how to manage and subdue my passions; I am comfortable expressing love in every aspect of life; I have cast off all fear contrary to love; I am excited about pursuing my purpose; and I am not ruled by anger.
___ 2) I am out of balance with regard to at least one of these four variables.
___ 3) I am out of balance with regard to at least two of these four variables.
___ 4) I am out of balance with regard to at least three of these four variables.

Emotional health (feelings) examples: love (Matt. 22:37), anger (Eph. 4:26), happiness (1 Pet. 4:13), sadness (Ps. 119:28), excitement (Ps. 69:9), grief (Eccles. 1:18).

Economic health - But remember the Lord your God, for it is he who gives you the ability to produce wealth, and so confirms his covenant, which he swore to your ancestors, as it is today (*Deuteronomy 8:18*)

The fifth aspect of health to be assessed is economic health; which relates to one's finances. *Employment* status is a critical factor of economic health (Gen. 3:19). Having an income source is a priority for the mature man and his responsibility in support of himself and his family (2 Thess. 3:10). Focused resources are necessary when one is in pursuit of purpose (www.fulfilling-life-purpose.com). *Tithes and taxes* are two additional components of economic health (Luke 20:25). *Tithes* is that first 10 percent of your increase that goes toward the up-building of God's kingdom. The mature man allocates his resources in a manner that supports kingdom building (Mal. 3:8). Taxes are that portion of one's earnings that goes to the government (www.irs.gov). Christ said render unto Caesar that which belongs to Caesar and unto God that which belongs to God (Matt. 22:21). *Investment* is another component of economic health that is important to financial stewardship (Eccles. 11:1 and Gal. 6:7). It is important for an individual to work toward fulfillment of purpose and it is equally important for one to ensure his resources are working for him (www.bloomberg.com/personal-finance/calculators). *Credit* is a component of one's financial stewardship that is rated based on the US financial system's confidence in an individual's likelihood to pay his debts (www.consumercredit.com). A mature man uses wisdom and discretion as to whether he chooses to use his credit or not (Prov. 22:7).

Where are you in regard to your financial stewardship?

The key factors of economic health that will be assessed here are employment, tithes, taxes, investments, and credit. Use the descriptions above to assess each individual factor of economic health and rate your overall economic status. Check the numbered line that best represents your assessment of the personal economic factors mentioned.

8. When it comes to my economic health:

___ 1) I have a consistent income source; I diligently pay my tithes and taxes; I have a diversified investment portfolio; and I am debt free.
___ 2) I am out of balance with regard to at least one of these five variables.
___ 3) I am out of balance with regard to at least two of these five variables.
___ 4) I am out of balance with regard to at least three of these five variables.
___ 5) I am out of balance with regard to at least four of these five variables.

Economic health (finances)—money (Eccles. 10:19), credit (Prov. 22:7), debt (Matt. 6:12), investments (Matt. 25:15–28), insurance (Rom. 8:17), taxes (Luke 20:25), etc…

Spiritual Health - God is spirit, and his worshipers must worship in the Spirit and in truth." (John *4:24*)

The sixth and final aspect of health to be assessed is spiritual health; which relates to one's soul and spirit. The key elements of spiritual health that will be assessed here are studying the word of God, prayer and fasting, faith, and the sharing of the Gospel of Jesus Christ. *Studying the Word of God* is a key element in the pursuit of spiritual identity and life purpose. Studying the word of God, as well as, studying the specific area of discipline related to your calling within the context of the word of God is paramount for the mature man (2 Tim. 2:15). Studying is crucial to acquiring knowledge to getting understanding, and to gaining wisdom of a specific subject matter (www.studygs.net). Studying enables the mature individual to love and worship the Lord with his mind (Luke 10:27). The next component of spiritual health to be assessed is prayer (1 Thess. 5:17). *Prayer* is communication with God. In order for men to develop intimacy with God they must pray (Luke 18:1). Jesus Christ gives instruction on how a mature man should pray (Matt. 6:9–13). Using scripture to pray in faith demonstrates one's agreement with God's word and guarantees a beneficial outcome for the mature man. *Fasting* is a component of spiritual health to be assessed. Fasting is abstaining from some food and/or drink for religious observance (www.sentara.com). The purpose of fasting is twofold, in that, it allows time for the cleaning and rejuvenation of the body (Matt. 17:21). It also enables the spiritual man time to be fed and be strengthened in order to keep the natural man under subjection. This twofold purpose allows the mature man to focus on who he is and to use his time and resources on fulfillment of purpose (Isa. 58). I would submit to you that *faith* is the seventh level of learning wherein knowledge is perfected (Heb. 11:1) and without faith, it is impossible to please God. Meaning, after an individual has experienced a body of knowledge at each of the other six levels of learning he has the opportunity to perfect his knowledge of that particular content through faith. Faith is that portion of our mental capacity that is often used the least. An example of this idea can be understood better through the analogy of learning to ride a bike. The final element of spiritual health is *ministry* (Matt. 28:19 and 20), which is the opportunity to meet the needs of people while extending the gospel of Jesus Christ. The mature man is constantly in the mode of ministry whether it is in his role as a husband, a father, a leader, and/or as a mentor.

The key components of spiritual health that will be assessed here are studying the word of God, prayer, fasting, faith, and ministry. Use the previous descriptions to assess each element of your spiritual health status. Check the numbered line below that best represents your assessment of the spiritual elements shared as they relate to your life.

9. When it comes to my spiritual health,

___1) I have studied to be affirmed by God, I regularly communicate with God through prayer, fasting is a crucial element in my spiritual life, I intentionally nurture my faith in God, and I daily look for ways to meet the needs of others.

___ 2) I am out of balance with regard to at least one of these five elements.

___ 3) I am out of balance with regard to at least two of these five elements.

___ 4) I am out of balance with regard to at least three of these five elements.

___ 5) I am out of balance with regard to at least four of these five elements.

Spiritual health (the soul)—beliefs (Rom. 10:8–10), morals, and values (Gal. 5), Matt. 6:33.

The Worker, the Warrior, and the Worshiper (Eccles. 12:13)

A mature man is one who *provides* for the needs of others, he *protects* against evil, and he is *the priest in his home* that serves the Lord in spirit and in truth.

In this section you have the opportunity to assess where you are in accordance with the duties of man. There are three things we are going to mention concerning the duties of man. The scriptures are clear about the duties and responsibilities of a man to God, to his wife, to his children, to his neighbor, to widows, and to orphans. Every man has a duty to work and provide for his household and community! Every man has a duty to war and protect those within his household and community! Every man has a duty to lead his household and others in worship! We are going to talk about these three things really quickly, so brace yourself like a man (Job 38:3). So there is no sidestepping; there is no getting away or around it. You have got to respond to these manly duties. The overarching question again is where are you, man? Where are you when it comes to fulfilling your duties as a man? The follow-up question is "Are you a mature man?" I'd like to remind you that these questions are being asked so that every man can examine himself. These are the questions to ponder as you reflect and meditate on your life with a scriptural context. Do you go hard after fulfillment of these duties? Or are you going hard after other things and being distracted from your manly duties. Do you understand what you are going hard after? And as a mature man, you should be going hard after the fulfillment of these duties? I challenge you to think about that question, I want you to ponder this question in terms of the worker, the warrior, and the worshiper.

Where are you as a man in regard to your duty to work, your duty to war, and your duty to worship?

10. As far as being a *worker* (Gen. 3:19, John 9:4, 2 Thess. 3:10),

____ 1) I am consistently working to fulfill my purpose in life, as well as, working to fulfill the needs of my family.

__ 2) I am often working to fulfill my purpose in life, as well as, working to fulfill the needs of my family.

__ 3) I am sometimes working to fulfill my purpose in life, as well as, working to fulfill the needs of my family.

__ 4) I am neither working to fulfill my purpose in life, nor am I working to fulfill the needs of my family.

11. As far as being a *warrior* (Eph. 6:13, 2 Cor. 10:4, and Mark 3:27):

__ 1) I am fully equipped with the whole armor of God, and I consistently engage in spiritual warfare.

__ 2) I am equipped with the whole armor of God, and I engage often in spiritual warfare.

__ 3) I know what the armor of God is, and I sometimes engage in spiritual warfare.

__ 4) I do not know what the armor of God is, and I do not understand spiritual warfare.

12. As far as being a *worshiper* (John 4:24, 1 Chron. 16:29, and Matt. 22:37),

__ 1) I consistently worship the Lord in spirit and in truth; in addition, I worship the Lord wholly with my heart, mind, body, soul, and finances.

__ 2) I often worship the Lord in spirit and in truth, in addition, I worship the Lord wholly with my heart, mind, body, soul, and finances.

__ 3) I sometimes worship the Lord in spirit and in truth, in addition, I worship the Lord wholly with my heart, mind, body, soul, and finances.

__ 4) I have not worshipped the Lord in spirit and in truth; neither have I worshipped the Lord with my heart, mind, body, soul and finances.

A mature man has a *vision* for fulfilling *his life's* purpose, for the direction of *his family (Joshua 24:15),* and for *his community.* A mature man loves, protects, encourages, and supports those around him, while he *teaches*, *trains*, and *imparts wisdom*.

13. When it comes to being a *husband* (Eph. 5:25, 1 Pet. 3:7, and Col. 3:19),

___ 1) I love my wife as Christ loves the church and I live with her according to a thorough and participatory knowledge of God (1 John 4–8 and 18).

___ 2) I love my wife and I live with her according to my understanding of a husband's role.

___ 3) I love my wife and I live with her according to my obligation as a husband.

___ 4) I have never been married, or I am divorced from my wife.

14. When it comes to being a *father* (Prov. 22:6, Eph. 6:4, and 2 Tim. 3:16–17):

___ 1) I love, protect, encourage, support, train, and affirm my children; I am teaching my children according to God's plan for their lives; and I am providing them opportunities to develop the gifts and talents God has given them.

__ 2) I am fulfilling two of the three variables mentioned above.

__ 3) I am fulfilling one of the three variables mentioned above.

__ 4) I am not a father, or I do not have a relationship with my children.

15. When it comes to being a *leader* (Matt. 23:11, Rom. 12:2–8, 2 Tim. 2:15, and 1 Tim. 3:2),

__1) I am a service-driven leader; I use the wisdom, knowledge, and understanding of the Holy Spirit to make decisions; I have been proven according to the call of God on my life; and I am blameless, the husband of one wife; vigilant, sober, of good behavior, given to hospitality, and apt to teach.

__2) I am fulfilling five to seven of the ten variables above.

__3) I am fulfilling four or less of the ten variables above.

__4) I do not see myself as a leader in any aspect of my life.

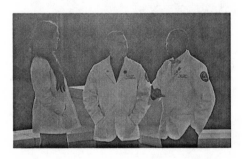

16. When it comes to being a *mentor* (Prov. 13:20, Prov. 27:17, Prov. 20:6, Eccles. 4:9, Prov. 15:22, Amos 3:3, and Ps. 15:2),

__ 1) I associate with men given to wisdom; I partner with faithful men; I strive to sharpen the countenance of the men with whom I am in fellowship with; I seek counsel from Godly men; I walk in agreement with men who are in agreement with God.

__ 2) I am fulfilling four of the five variables above.

__ 3) I am fulfilling three or less of the five variables above.

__ 4) I am not a mentor, nor do I have a mentor.

The Measure of a Man [162]

Tally up the scores assigned to each of the sixteen items previously assessed to determine your overall maturity rating. Your overall score will fall within a range of numbers to give an indication of where you are as a man in the process of maturity.

1. __	2. __	3. __	4. __
5. __	6. __	7. __	8. __
9. __	10. __	11. __	12. __
13. __	14. __	15. __	16. __

Total Score (1 through 16)

I am a mature man	-	1–22
I am a maturing man	-	23–44
I am an immature man	-	45–66

As you review your assessments for each aspect of your life, you should consider both your areas of strength and your areas for improvement. Identify your areas of strength in order to encourage yourself and develop a plan as to how you will maintain those areas.

---

[162] **Ephesians 4:13** "Till we all come in the unity of the faith, and of the knowledge of the Son of God, unto a perfect man, unto the measure of the stature of the fullness of Christ."

Likewise, you must identify those areas that need improvement and create goals for your personal wellness plan (see appendix A) in support of each aspect of your personal life. So, I speak to the spirit of every man who has engaged this message in some way…lay aside the weights, the sin, and the distractions in your life. Let perseverance finish its work so that you may be mature and complete, not lacking anything.[163] Not lacking in faith, not lacking in the knowledge of God, not lacking in fidelity, and not lacking in integrity. Yet, full of love, full of care, full of truth, disciplined, upright, sober-minded, respectable, and able to teach.

Come on, man of God! I encourage you to go forth and strengthen your body and your mind; while establishing the appropriate relationships, subduing your passions, as well as, prospering both spiritually and naturally (in that order). We have previously defined maturity as, "the result of drawing closer to God when one's spiritual identity and life purpose come into alignment." I declare to you, that a mature man will tell the *truth in love*. The mature man lives out his life using the gifts and talents he has developed to fulfill his purpose within the great commission. May the love of God, the grace of our Lord Jesus, and the sweet communion of the Holy Spirit rest, rule, and abide with you always, I pray, in the name of the Father, the Son, and the Holy Spirit. Amen!

---

[163]   James 1:4

Figure: Mature Man Wordle (A to Z)

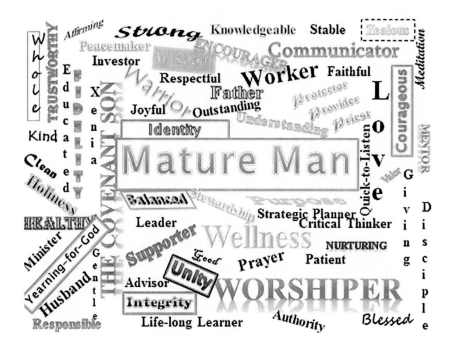

Reference

Bee, H. L. (1992). *The developing child* (6th ed.). New York, NY: HarperCollins College Publishers.

Bible Gateway, retrieved from http://www.biblegateway.com.

Blooms, B. S. (1956). *Taxonomy of Educational Objectives, Handbook I: The Cognitive Domain.* New York: David McKay Co Inc.

Erikson, E. (1959). *Identity and the life cycle.* New York, NY: Norton.

Erikson, E. (1968). *Identity: Youth and crisis.* New York, NY: Norton.

Free Dictionary, http://www.thefreedictionary.com/maturity

Hatcher, J. H. (2011). The African-American Adolescent Male

Identity Development Crisis: A Mixed-Methods Design Exploring the Relationship Between Ethnic Identity Development Status and Student Achievement. Regent University, VA. Dissertation. Retrieved from http://www.regent.edu/acad/schedu/pdfs/abstracts/hatcher_2011.pdf.

Eldredge, J. (2009). Fathered by God: Learning What Your Dad Could Never Teach You.

Maslow, A. (1946). A theory of human motivation. *Psychological Review, 50,* 370–396.

Maslow, A. (1954). *Motivation and personality.* New York, NY: Harper. Maslow, A. (1954). *Motivation and personality.* New York: Harper.

Meriam-Wester, www.meriam-webster.com

Miller, P. H. (2002). *Theories of developmental psychology* (4th ed.). New York, NY: Worth.

LifeWay Biblical Solutions for Life, http://www.lifeway.com/lwc/files/lwcF_PDF_DSC_Spiritual_Growth_Assessment.pdf Nelson, Thomas, Inc.

Ramsey, D. (2016). www.daveramsey.com

The Critical Thinking Foundation

The Sleep Foundation, http://www.sleepfoundation.org/article/how-sleep-works/how-much-sleep-do-we-really-need

GLOSSARY

A

Anger: a negative emotion and spirit that is rooted in fear that is commonly expressed by immature people.

C

Covenant: the most intimate type of relationship and is established by a spoken and/or written vow.

D

Death: separation from God and His divine order.

Discipleship: to teach and train according to the words of Jesus Christ.

Discipline: strict adherence to God's instructions.

Disobedience: Any action contrary to God's law and His instructions; failure to obey God's word.

F

Faith: trust that is rooted in love: it is a spiritual and a perfected knowledge; it is the highest level of learning.

Fasting: is a spiritual exercise whereby one denies his natural desires and focuses on his spiritual needs. Feeding your faith and starving doubt (IB).

Fatherhood: The covenant relationship between a man and his child (or children); the man responsible for loving, protecting, encouraging, supporting, training, and affirming his child (or children); he speaks into the life of his child while guiding him/her toward discovery of their spiritual identity and fulfillment of their life's purpose.

Father Wound: Is the deepest wound a person can carry. The father found s an offense to a child potentially in any aspect of their being; which results from the absence of fathering; or the failure of the father to meet the child's needs; it can result in one or more of the following: abuse, low self-esteem, feelings of rejection, low academic achievement, and abandonment, poverty, identity crisis, and much, much more; it is also the result of a child not receiving the love, protection, encouragement, support, training, and affirmation, a child needs from their father (Eldridge, 2011; Hatcher, 2015).

Fear: Fear is a spirit that is contrary to Love; it is rooted in all that is evil.

Fidelity: the quality of being faithful or loyal that is rooted in love; it enables one to maintain the intimacy of a covenant relationship.

G

Guilt: the feeling a person might experience when they are at fault; it is blame assigned to one who has engaged in a wrongful act; and it is a negative response to a developmental crisis; a conscientiousness of wrong doing.

H

Health: the quality of life that relates to one's body, mind, relationships, feelings, finances, soul, and spirit.

Holiness: a lifestyle by which one lives in strict obedience to God's word and in His righteousness.

Husband: the man who enters into a covenant relationship with a woman and becomes responsible for loving, protecting, encouraging, and supporting her; he is to be the band around and covering for their household; he is the head of household; the strong man; the man that becomes one physically, mentally, socially, emotionally, economically, and spiritually with a woman.

Hygiene: the daily practice of cleansing the body for the purpose of ridding the body of germs and disease causing agents.

I

Identity: a predetermined role one has been created to assume in the plan of God; the genetic encoding; and that which is aligned to one's life purpose. One's identity is the spiritual download that God performed in the spirit realm at the beginning of time.

Illness: is any sickness, disease, dysfunction, disorder, disruption as it relates to any/or all aspects of one's being.

Integrity: the wholeness and alignment of one's truest spiritual identity and their life's purpose; it will manifest itself in both their personal and public life.

Investments: initial resources given with the expectation of a greater return.

L

Leader: the person responsible for serving, training, and commissioning others toward fulfillment of the Great Commission.

Learning: the process of acquiring knowledge, developing skills, and promoting attitudes that support the discovery one's spiritual identity and the fulfillment of one's life's purpose.

Love: Love is God and God is *love*; it is the source of all that exists.

M

Maturity: the result of drawing closer to God; it is when one's spiritual identity comes into alignment with one's life purpose.

Meditation: a mental exercise that involves deep and deliberate reflecting and focusing on God's word.

Mentor: the person in a committed or covenant relationship responsible for guiding someone who is less experienced toward discovering their spiritual identity, development of their gifts and talents, and fulfillment of their life's purpose.

Ministry: An opportunity to meet the needs of people in a way that aligns with God's word.

O

Obedience: actions that are aligned with the instructions given by God the Father through His word and/or through the Holy Spirit.

P

Prayer: sincere communication with God the Father through the Lord Jesus Christ that is expressed spiritually and/or verbally.

Purpose: the spiritual assignment of one's life; the predestined call on one's life.

R

Resilience: the will to be restored to one's original place; the ability to bounce back from a setback.

Respect: to treat someone the way you desire to be treated; to give honor; show appreciation; the quality of admiration of another.

Responsibility: one's ability to act or react in accordance with God's word to the duties and expectations ascribed to the various roles to which we are assigned.

Rest: a pause or slowing of the normal functioning of one's body, mind, and/or soul; a time of rejuvenation.

S

Salvation (to be saved): to repent and to be reconciled with God; to re-establish God's intended relationship with man; and to be delivered from God's judgment and wrath.

Shame: the dishonor, disgrace, and embarrassment that a person may experience; a result of a conscientiousness of sin or wrong doing.

Sin: actions that are contrary to God's law, His instructions, His commandments, and His ordinances.

Son: Those who have believed on the name of Jesus and have accepted Him as their Lord and savior.

Strategic planning: a mental exercise that involves developing and organizing the steps and processes necessary to accomplish a goal.

Studying: a mental exercise that involves actively engaging the word of God in order to discover one's spiritual identity, as well as, to fulfill one's life's purpose.

U

Unity: an orderly system; parts that are fitly joined and working together on one accord for one purpose.

W

Warrior: one who fights for love and against spiritual wickedness; he protects everyone and everything given to his charge.

Wellness: the highest quality of health one can achieve to include each of the six aspects of one's being (e.g. physical, mental, social, emotional, economical, & spiritual).

Wholeness: the sum of one; not lacking any parts; complete and together; fitly joined; representing a state of complex unity.

Worker: one who labors for the cause of Christ; a person who extends the necessary efforts toward fulfillment of the Great Commission (Matt. 28:19 and 20).

Worshiper: one who experiences God in spirit and in truth with every spiritual sense; he yields his whole mind, his whole heart, and his whole body to the Lord's good pleasure.

APPENDIX A

Personal Wellness Plan (PWP)

*Commit to the Lord whatever you do, and he
will establish your plans (Prov. 16:3).*

*"For I know the plans I have for you," declares the
Lord, "plans to prosper you and not to harm you, plans
to give you hope and a future" (Jer. 29:11).*

*Then the Lord replied write down the vision and
make it plain on tablets…(Habbakuh 2:2)*

The personal wellness plan (PWP) assignment that I am sharing with
you now is very important action step towards ensuring that your goals
and aspirations are aligned with God's plan and purpose for your life.
God has given each of us a vision for our life by uploading our identity
in the spirit realm. You can see it. It may be cloudy; it may not be

clear but you can see what God has for you. The Personal Wellness Plan is a written plan that reflects your personal goals. The PWP has a dual purpose. The first purpose of the PWP is to ensure that your personal goals are aligned with the plans and purpose that God has for your life. The second purpose for this plan of goals is to promote your personal health in each aspect of your life as you develop and mature toward the discovery of your spiritual identity and as you move closer to fulfillment of your life's purpose. The Word of God declares that we should write the vision and make it plain. Every man should have a vision for his personal life, a vision for his family, and a vision for his ministry. To give an analogy, it is like an architect who has the vision for building a house. The architect must write the vision in the form of a blueprint in order to get the appropriate approval (2 Tim. 2:15) and to get the necessary assistance with the construction of the house. The PWP is a living document that will be modified as you mature and the plan of God becomes clearer in your life. Clarity also comes as the result of goals being set and accomplished and as new goals are written. These goals are steps closer to God's plan and purpose for you.

The PWP goals are developed by the person for whom they are written. The goals are written using the MAPS criteria; which requires the written goals to be *m*easurable, *a*ttainable, *p*ersonal, and *s*pecific. Measurable denotes the ability to gauge whether you have achieved your goal or not. So, if I set a goal that I would like to accomplish by a certain date, I would use a calendar to assess where I am in relation to my goal. Attainable meaning it is realistic and it is something that you can accomplish. If my son, at age fourteen, set a goal to have his driver's license in six months that would not be attainable, because of the age requirements for driving in our state. It has to be personal, which implies something you desire to accomplish for yourself. It should not be a goal that someone else has created for you without you owning it. It is a personal goal it is a goal that you desire to have manifested in your life. That is why it is called a Personal Wellness Plan. The "S" stands for specific, meaning it has to have detail. The more detail your goal statement includes the clearer it will be and the more likely it will be that you accomplish the goal. Below you will find a mental health goal using the MAPS criteria.

I recommend that you start with three (3) goals for each of the six (6) aspects of health, which will give you a minimum 18 goals to start. In addition, each goal should be supported by scriptural text; which ensures alignment with God's word and His plan for you. There are three steps in this goal writing process for the PWP and they are as follows:

1) Write out the goal statement, which states where you desire to go.
2) Write a reference statement that indicates where you are now in relationship to the stated goal.
3) Write an explanation of what steps you will take in order to accomplish the goal.

- My goal is to graduate with a doctoral degree in Educational Leadership from Regent University by the end of 2010 (*see further detail about this goal under the mental health example below*).

The stated goal is measurable by identifying the type of degree, the level of the degree, where the degree is to be acquired, and the year by which it is to be obtained. The goal was attainable because the degree program included two years of course work and an additional five year period of time within which to complete the research dissertation (the program was started in 2006). I need to interject that this goal was also attainable because I was blessed to receive a fellowship that paid 100% of my tuition and I was also paid a $10,000 stipend for three years. God did exceedingly and abundantly above all I asked or thought was possible. This goal was personal because it was my desire to further develop myself as an educator. Finally, the details of the goal highlight the specificity of the goal and made it more likely that I would stay focused and accomplish the goal. If you have ever been to a mall that you are unfamiliar with you will usually look for the marquee with a directory and a layout of floor plans. The reference statement portion of the assignment is like the red dot on the marquee that holds the mall's directory and states, "You are here."

The explanation in this scenario would be the actual steps you plan out in order to get to the store(s) where you desire to go.

Personal wellness is a vital part of our growth, development, and ultimate maturity in life. It is something that we must give time and attention to on a daily basis. There is a delicate balance that is necessary for every individual to achieve the highest levels of health in each of the six aspects of life. As you begin to write your wellness plan, keep in mind that you are writing goals to align your will with God's will for you. In addition, these goals are to develop and manage the health of your body, your mind, your relationships, your feelings, your finances, your soul and spirit. All goals are written out because they become a blueprint for your vision. Writing out your goals adds another level of commitment to the desired outcomes. It also becomes a guide for yourself and those who would assist you with accomplishing your goals. You must understand that if a goal only remains a thought or a spoken word it is only a wish until you declare it and write it down. A wish is a casual thought whereas a goal requires another level of commitment.

It is important to have scriptures to which your goals align. Why? Because, we want our plan to align with God's plan for us. We don't want to set goals that we think are good for us and discover afterward that they are not according to God's plan. We want our lives to align with the word of God as we become living epistles and mature Christians. So, this is not an assignment that you are just going to do half-heartedly. It may take you two weeks, a month, maybe six months, or even a year of prayer, study, and meditation on the word of God and communing with the Holy Spirit in order to complete this work. This is a plan of how you will live out your life according to God's plan for you. As you set your goals and you align them with God's word, I pray that the Holy Spirit will give you an unction to complete the work that the Lord has begun in you. As you accomplish these goals what God has for you is going to become more and more clear. It is clear to me now. When it is clear to you, you can walk in the integrity and holiness (wholeness) that the Lord expects from a mature man. No wavering. No doubting. You can walk in it. You become the living word of God! Hallelujah! This is the holiness and integrity that every man should aspire to. When you are walking in the word of God, you are walking in holiness, you are on point, you are where you are supposed to be, you are doing what He has instructed you to do.

Man of God, I pray in the name of Jesus Christ that you would be healed, made whole, and that you would live a well-balanced life full of the abundance of God's best for you! I challenge you my brother in the name of Jesus Christ to finish what you have started and *live well!*

Personal Wellness Plan (PWP)

Criteria for each goal:

Scriptural Reference – You can start by having an overall scriptural reference for your PWP. A scripture is used to demonstrate alignment between God's plan for you and the goals you have set. So, each goal should also align with a relevant scripture. For me, that scripture is 3 John: 2 which states, *"Beloved I wish above all things that you would proper and be in health even as your soul prospers."* In addition, every goal must meet the MAPS standard: (M) measurable, (A) attainable, (P) personal, and (S) specific. The reference statement is the result of the assessment of where you are in regard to the stated goal. It shows your current location like a GPS system. It lets you know where you are in proximity to where you need to be. The explanation represents the steps that will be taken in order to get from where you are to the achievement of the goal. I have included a rubric at the end for you to assess yourself.

Let us get started!

The following notes are examples from my personal wellness plan:

Physical Health (*The Body*) 1 Corinthians 6:15a – Know ye not that your bodies are the members of Christ?

1a. Goal Statement (Hebrews 12:1) – Lay aside the weight
My goal is to keep my weight between 205 lbs. and 210 lbs. on a consistent basis by January 2015.
b. Reference Statement –
As of May 2014 I weighed in at 247 lbs; I consume GMO food products; and I average six to seven hours of sleep per night.
c. Explanation –
I will use my YMCA membership to play raquetball two *to three times per week; convert to eating organic food* products; and get seven to eight hours of sleep nightly.

2a. Goal Statement (*Scripture*) –
_____
_____

b. Reference Statement –
_____
_____

c. Explanation –
_____
_____

3a. Goal Statement (*Scripture*) -
_____
_____

b. Reference Statement -
_____
_____

c. Explanation -
_____
_____

Mental Health (*The Mind*) Romans 12:2 – Do not conform to the pattern of this world, but be transformed by the renewing of your mind, then you will be able to test and prove what God's will is – His good, pleasing, and perfect will.

> **1a. Goal Statement** (*2 Tim. 2:15*)
> My goal is to graduate with a doctoral degree in Educational Leadership from Regent University by the end of 2010. Written by JWH3 2006
> **b. Reference Statement** –
> At the present time (February 2006), I have a master's degree in Education Administration and I am starting the process for admission into the doctoral program at Regent University.
> **c. Explanation** –
> I will complete the admissions packet on-time and once accepted I will take the appropriate course of study, then take the comprehensive exams, and finally complete the dissertation.
>
> **2a.** Goal Statement (*Scripture*) –
> _____
> _____
>
> **b.** Reference Statement –
> _____
> _____
>
> **c.** Explanation –
> _____
> _____
>
> **3a.** Goal Statement (Scripture) -
> _____
> _____
>
> **b.** Reference Statement -
> _____
> _____
>
> **c.** Explanation -
> _____
> _____

Social Health (*Relationships*) Matthew 22:36–40 – Teacher, which is the greatest commandment in the law. Jesus replied, love the Lord your God with all your heart, and with all your soul, and with all your mind. This is the first and greatest commandment. The second is like it, love your neighbor as yourself. All the law and the prophets hang on these two commandments.

1a. Goal Statement (*Scripture*) –

_____

_____

b. Reference Statement –

_____

_____

c. Explanation –

_____

_____

2a. Goal Statement (*Scripture*) –

_____

_____

b. Reference Statement –

_____

_____

c. Explanation –

_____

_____

3a. Goal Statement (*Scripture*) -

_____

_____

b. Reference Statement -

_____

_____

c. Explanation -

_____

_____

Emotional Health (*Feelings*) **Galatians 5:24** – Those who belong to Jesus Christ have crucified the flesh with its passions and desires.

1a. Goal Statement (*Scripture*) -

_____

_____

b. Reference Statement –

_____

_____

c. Explanation –

_____

_____

2a. Goal Statement (*Scripture*) –

_____

_____

b. Reference Statement –

_____

_____

c. Explanation –

_____

_____

3a. Goal Statement (*Scripture*) -

_____

_____

b. Reference Statement -

_____

_____

c. Explanation -

_____

_____

Economic health (*Finances*) Ecclesiastes 11:1 – Cast thy bread upon the waters: for thou shalt find it after many days.

1a. Goal Statement (*Scripture*) -

_____

_____

b. Reference Statement –

_____

_____

c. Explanation –

_____

_____

2a. Goal Statement (Scripture) –

_____

_____

b. Reference Statement –

_____

_____

c. Explanation –

_____

_____

3a. Goal Statement (Scripture) -

_____

_____

b. Reference Statement -

_____

_____

c. Explanation -

_____

_____

Spiritual Health (*The Soul and Spirit*) **John 4:24** – God is spirit and His worshipers must worship in spirit and in truth.

1a. Goal Statement (*Scripture*) –

_____

_____

b. Reference Statement –

_____

_____

c. Explanation –

_____

_____

2a. Goal Statement (*Scripture*) –

_____

_____

b. Reference Statement –

_____

_____

c. Explanation –

_____

_____

3a. Goal Statement (*Scripture*) -

_____

_____

b. Reference Statement -

_____

_____

c. Explanation -

_____

_____

Personal Wellness Plan Rubric

	Exceeds Standard (4)	Meets Standard (3)	Below Standard (2)	Needs Improvement (1)
Do your goals meet the M.A.P.S. criteria?	My goals are measurable, attainable, personal, and specific; they are very clear and detailed.	My goals are measurable, attainable, personal, and specific.	My goals meet 3 out of the 4 criterions	My goals meet 2 or less of the 4 criterions.
Do you have a scripture reference for your personal identity and purpose?	I have a scripture reference for my personal identity and purpose that is clear and relevant to my life.	I have a scripture reference for my personal identity and purpose.	I am unsure about the scripture reference for my personal identity and purpose.	I do not have a scripture reference for my personal identity and purpose.
Do you have a scripture reference for each goal statement?	I have multiple scripture references for each of my goals and I understand clearly how they are connected.	I have a scripture reference that is connected to each of my goals.	There is no clear connection between the scriptures used and each of my goals.	I do not have a scripture reference for each of my stated goals.
Do you have (3) Goals for each aspect of health?	I have more than 3 goals for each aspect of health.	I have a minimum of 3 goals for each aspect of health	There are 2 or less goals for each aspect of health	I do not have a goal statement for 1 or more aspects of health
Do you have a reference statement that indicates "where you are" in reference to each goal?	I have a clear and detailed reference statement that indicates "where I am" in reference to each goal.	I have a reference statement that indicates *"where I am"* in reference to each of my goals.	I have some unclear reference statements about "where I am" in reference to some of my goals.	I do not have a reference statement that indicates "where I am" in reference to each of my goals.
Do you have an explanation of the steps to be taken to achieve each goal?	I have clear and detailed statements explaining the steps to be taken in order to achieve each goal.	I have statements explaining the steps to be taken in order to achieve each goal.	I have some unclear explanations about the steps to be taken in order to achieve some of my goals.	I do not have an explanation of the steps to be taken to achieve each goal.

APPENDIX B

Men Who Fathered Me

John Eldridge wrote, "A boy becomes a man only through the active intervention of his father and the fellowship of men. It cannot happen any other way."

My father, *John Wills Hatcher Jr.*, taught me many things about being a man. A few of the main takeaways from him were that a man provides for his family, a man protects his family, and a man should always use common sense. He also taught me about the attributes of a leader. My father was a disabled veteran with two plastic hips from being a paratrooper in the United States Army during the Korean War. Although he was considered more than 50 percent disabled he would, at times, get up around three thirty or four o'clock in the morning and go to work on a local garbage truck in order to make sure we had food to eat. When I consider this point now I can hear him say, "A man has got to do what a man has got to do!" My father explained to me that although I was the youngest child, it was my responsibility to look after my youngest sister while we were in school. He even went as far as to say if something happened to her and I didn't do something then I would have to answer to him. When she finally left home he sent me to check on her and to make sure she was fine. I was responsible for protecting her until she got married and even after that I needed to check on her. Common sense was another important concept that my father stressed. He never graduated from high school but, he could take $20 back in the mid-1980s and buy a few meals that could stretch for about a week using my mother's culinary skills. What I think my father developed as a result of his life experiences was the ability to think critically about a variety of topics and encouraged me to do the same. Finally, my father shared his idea of leadership by stating that leaders know how to, "improvise, advise, delegate, and organize." I remember working with my father at times doing odd jobs; while doing so I was afforded the opportunity to experience his leadership philosophy first hand. There were many lessons, such as, providing and protecting family that my father taught me; however, these are the most significant to being a mature man.

My father lived until I was 17 years old and a seamen recruit in the United States Navy. I was three weeks into boot camp when I received the message from the chaplain that my father had passed. The two months between my graduation from high school and leaving for boot camp my father and I spent hours talking about life. I remember at one point he asked my mother to leave the room while we talked. I didn't realize it at the time but my father was sharing with me the duties of a man, as he understood it. Although I cannot remember every conversation verbatim, I believe that time with my father has had a profound impact on my life.

My paternal grandfather, *John Wills Hatcher Sr.*, was an example of a worker and a steward over his finances. Grand-pop retired from the Merck Corporation after thirty years of service as a custodian. His ability to maintain employment with the same company and achieve longevity is a testament to his work ethic. He retired with a monthly pension and a gold watch; which had an impression on me as a boy. Grand-pop didn't have any debts, he paid for whatever he purchased with cash, and the quality of the items he did purchase was very important to him. Grand-pop viewed his purchases as investments. He established and situated himself as a financial resource in our family by working hard and managing his finances in a way that enabled him to be the lender and not the borrower.

My maternal step-grandfather, *Curtis Crum Sr.*, was a man who loved his family and taught us the importance of protecting our family. He was a big man with a big heart and he had the heart of a lion. As a boy I recall him instructing the older family members to look out for the younger members and the male members were to protect the female members. He would organize outings and events designed to bring the family together. Granddad taught us that it was important for family to know one another and to stay connected to one another.

The man I consider to be my spiritual father is the late *Reverend Junius Callands*. He was the pastor of the House of Refuge Church in Elizabeth New Jersey; which is where I was born. Our family eventually moved to Plainfield New Jersey and the House of Refuge church eventually moved to Newark New Jersey; however, Rev. Callands continued to pick up my brother, my youngest sister, and I for church every week. The spiritual songs, the Sunday school lessons, the preached word of God, and the fellowship he provided demonstrated the love of God. Rev. Callands's example led me to received salvation at the age of 15.

My "father-in-love" *Reverend William H. Green* was an example of a man who was the spiritual leader in his family. Big Pop was a man given to prayer, he had healing in his hands. He had the gift of helps and he was a master builder. Anyone who spent time with Big Pop would quickly become a part of his prayer life whether through conversation or a working relationship with him as he talked with the Holy Spirit. Through his ministry he would discern sickness, call it out by name, lay hands on the individual, and they would recover. Anywhere he went he would stop to help someone along the way who was in need. I would say of all the things he built in his lifetime, Big Pop's masterpiece has got to be his family.

Reverend Lawrence Wyatt was my pastor after coming home from the military and he is the man who counseled and married April and I. Rev. Wyatt was very instrumental in my spiritual maturity as he taught and told stories. He would often say things like, "he said, she said, but what does God say" and "get all you can, and can all you get." Rev. Wyatt would use sayings like these and stories to teach life lessons.

Mr. Alfred Myers a.k.a. Big Al is the man I call my Italian father. I met Big Al being stationed overseas in Sigonella, Italy, while in the US Navy. He helped me at a critical point in my early manhood after my father passed. Big Al helped me get acclimated to the Italian culture and he also helped me sharpen my skills as a young racquetballer. I was nineteen years old and Big Al allowed me to come into his trailer office and glean from his experience as a retired Army drill sergeant. He and his wife Giovanna (my Italian mother) invited me into their home from time to time and treated me like a son. I am forever grateful to them both for their love and kindness towards me. As a man in his retirement years Big Al was and is an example a mature man who has maintained great physical health. He is the only man among these men who helped me mature into man that is still alive. I believe it is very interesting given he is the only one from whom I was able to see an example of great physical health.

Man Training

John Wills "John-John" Hatcher IV

I have been telling my son, since the age of one that, "there is a king in you!" He started watching the Disney movie *The Lion King* over and over again trying to satisfy his curiosity about what I was telling him. We started playing chess when he was about five years old to reinforce the lesson about protecting your king and knowing your personal identity. We continued to play chess throughout his younger years and on occasion we would still watch the "The Lion King" movie, but most importantly he understands now that the King in him is the love of God, the King of kings…King Jesus!

Who are the **men** that have or who are fathering *you*? In what aspects of your life did they or are they fathering you?

GOD IS LOOKING FOR A MATURE MAN; WHERE ARE YOU MAN?

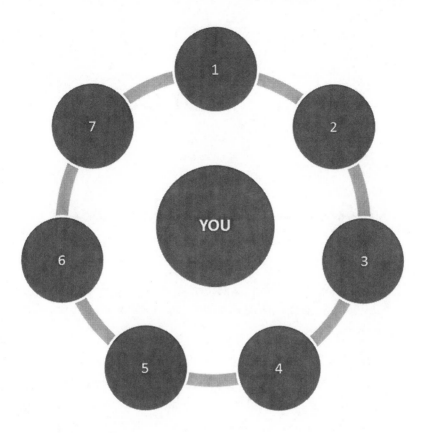

Additional questions:

1.   Who are you fathering?
2.   Who are you mentoring?
3.   Who are your mentors?

APPENDIX C

Nigerian Engagement Process

The process Dr. Ononiwu described is designed to admonish the two individuals considering marriage. He explained the process in the following steps:

> **Step 1.** When a man finds the woman he desires to marry he will first go to his father and inform his father (or a male elder if the father is deceased). The father will inquire about the son's ability to provide for himself and his own family. This is to avoid bringing shame on the father and his family because the son is unable to provide adequately for his wife and children.

> **Step 2.** When the father is satisfied that the son is financially prepared to provide for his family he will send a message to the father of the young woman who his son desires to marry and request a meeting. The father will also send a team to investigate the family and conduct background checks to make sure the young lady's family is not a part of a group of outcasts (or slaves). In addition, they will check for

any history of mental illness. When the meeting is set, the father will get a few (2 to 3) trusted elders, a jar of Palm wine, and go to meet with the father of the young lady.

Step 3. During this first meeting the young man's father will communicate to the father of the young lady that he has become aware of a flower that is growing in his garden. He will make a request to pluck the flower from his garden; to which the father of the young lady would ask what is the name of this flower? The response would be the young lady's name. The father of the young man and those who came with him would leave after the initial discussion and wait to hear from the father of the young lady within a week or two. If the father of the young lady is not interested he will not respond; however, if there is still interest a second meeting is scheduled.

Step 4. The second meeting takes place with a greater number of family members and elders from both sides (five or more from both sides). The father of the young man will bring enough palm wine for the larger group.

Step 5. After the second meeting the young lady is called before the family and extended family. She is admonished and counseled regarding the matter.

Step 6. A third meeting is scheduled, more palm wine is brought, and the young man's family brings gifts. During the third meeting the young lady is brought out and asked what her response is to the request for marriage. If her response is favorable she will leave with the young man's family and stay with his mother for two days.

Step 7. During the two day stay the family has the opportunity to observe her and she can observe the family. The young lady will get up in the morning and clean house and do household chores. After the two days are up the young lady is sent home with gifts or the process can end here.

Step 8. If things continue, the fourth meeting is scheduled with an even larger group (than the previous meeting) of family members and elders from both sides will attend. More palm wine and gifts are brought and there is a feast. It is during this meeting that the dowry and gifts are presented and discussed by the young lady's family. It is negotiated what the young man's family will bring to the wedding.

Step 9. After the fourth meeting the young lady again returns with the young man's family and spends four days with the mother of the young man observing his family and being observed by his family.

Step 10. A time is set for the young lady to go back for an eight day stay. Once that visit takes place the young lady comes back to let her father know she is ready. This is the point of no return.

Step 11. Negotiations continue during the wedding ceremony until the father of the bride determines he is satisfied and the marital vows are exchanged.

This process is to ensure both families feel comfortable with the union. The father of the bride requires the young man's family to invest in his daughter and the marriage itself. Both families, including the extended family members, the elders, and their communities become fully invested in this covenant union.

I believe there are some valuable insights here that can help to heal the breach in the current society's perceptions of the institution of marriage.

APPENDIX D

Character Profile of a Mature Man

Character Profile of a **Mature Man** –
(The balance between the **Lion** & the **Lamb**)

The character traits listed below and those found in the previous A to Z wordle (p. 136) represent a profile of a mature man. Examine these character traits and **(1).** Identify the 10 characteristics that you believe are the most important for the mature man, and explain why. **(2).** Now, circle the top three characteristics that you believe are the most important among the previous 10 and reflect on how you want those traits to be manifested in your life. **(3).** Add to the current list any characteristic you believe should be represented in the profile of a mature man (*use the other cell*).

Advisor	Encouraging	Nurturing
Affectionate	Expressive	Other: 1, 2, 3
Affirming	Gentle	Patient
Assertive	Giving	Positive Role Model
Balanced	Good Steward	Protector
Clean	Hard Working	Purpose Driven
Compassionate	Honest	Respectful
Confident	Hopeful	Responsible
Courageous	Humble	Spiritual
Covenant Keeper	Informed	Stable
Decisive	Integrity	Strong
Discerning	Kind	Supportive
Disciplined	Leader	Trustworthy
Educated	Life-long learner	Understanding
Effective communicator	Loving	Wisdom

*Additional paper needed

A Standard of Love (1 Corinthians 13)

If I speak with the tongues of men and of angels, but do not have *love*, I have become a noisy gong or a clanging cymbal. If I have the gift of prophecy, and know all mysteries and all knowledge; and if I have all faith, so as to remove mountains, but do not have *love*, I am nothing. And if I give all my possessions to feed the poor, and if I surrender my body to be burned, but do not have **love**, it profits me nothing. *Love is patient, love is kind and is not jealous; love does not brag and is not arrogant, (love) does not act unbecomingly; it does not seek its own, (love) is not provoked, (love) does not take into account a wrong suffered, (love) does not rejoice in unrighteousness, but rejoices with the truth; (love) bears all things, (love) believes all things, (love) hopes all things, (love) endures all things. Love never fails*; but if there are gifts of prophecy, they will be done away; if there are tongues, they will cease; if there is knowledge, it will be done away. For we know in part and we prophesy in part; but when the perfect comes, the partial will be done away. When I was a child, I used to speak like a child, think like a child, reason like a child; when I became *a man*, I did away with childish things. For now we see in a mirror dimly, but then face to face; now I know in part, but then I will know fully just as I also have been fully known. But now faith, hope, love, abide these three; but the greatest of these is *Love*.

The Mature Man's Declaration

I am a covenant Son of God, and I will love the Lord Jesus Christ with all my heart, mind, soul, and strength.

I am made whole by faith and through the love of Jesus Christ, and I will be an example of His love while leading my family and community.

I am created in the image of my heavenly Father, and I will work to fulfill His purpose in my life.

I am a soldier in the army of the Lord, and I will always fight for love and against spiritual wickedness.

I am a covenant worker, warrior, and worshipper; I will worship the Lord with reverence and awe and in spirit and truth, and in the beauty of holiness!!!

By God's grace, I declare that I am a mature man and that I will teach the full Gospel of Jesus Christ in love, truth, and with the integrity of the Holy Spirit!

Other Inspirational and Self-Help Resources

Fitness Test –
(www.adultfitness.org)

Spiritual Assessment http://www.lifeway.com/lwc/files/
lwcF_PDF_DSC_Spiritual_Growth_Assessment.pdf

Spiritual Gifts
http://www.spiritualgiftstest.com/

The Critical Thinking Foundation

To join the *Mature Man Covenant Brotherhood* or for booking workshops or training sessions contact us at:

www.thematureman.com or
By phone at (757) 286- 5723 or via
Facebook @ The Mature Man

Audios Book made available also in foreign languages.

ABOUT THE AUTHOR

Dr. John Wills Hatcher III is an ordained minister of the gospel of Jesus Christ. John has been married to his wife, April for more than 22 years and together they have reared their five Christian children. He is a veteran of the United States Navy and has served his country during the Dessert Storm war before receiving an honorable discharge. John received his doctorate in Educational Leadership from Regent University in Virginia Beach. He is a licensed teacher and has been an educational leader in both the public and private sectors from the elementary school level through the post-graduate level. He has published research on male identity development and his most recent study is in the area of character development among K-12 students. John has initiated the Sons of Promise and Daughters of Destiny tiered mentorship program in the context of schools, as well as, in community settings. He has also partnered with other leaders to engage mentorship opportunities for hundreds of young men and women in communities in New Jersey and Virginia. John continues to be a strong advocate for youth development and continuous "Man Training". He speaks in a variety of venues teaching about identity development, honing gifts and talents, and pursuing purpose in life. John is very passionate about his call to teach and he is honored and excited to share the message that God has laid on his heart.

CPSIA information can be obtained
at www.ICGtesting.com
Printed in the USA
LVOW08s0206060617
537064LV00001B/84/P